Learning Swift™ Programming

Addison-Wesley Learning Series

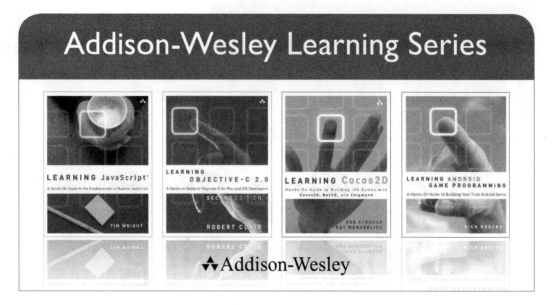

✦ Addison-Wesley

Visit informit.com/learningseries for a complete list of available publications.

The Addison-Wesley Learning Series is a collection of hands-on programming guides that help you quickly learn a new technology or language so you can apply what you've learned right away.

Each title comes with sample code for the application or applications built in the text. This code is fully annotated and can be reused in your own projects with no strings attached. Many chapters end with a series of exercises to encourage you to reexamine what you have just learned, and to tweak or adjust the code as a way of learning.

Titles in this series take a simple approach: they get you going right away and leave you with the ability to walk off and build your own application and apply the language or technology to whatever you are working on.

✦ Addison-Wesley   informIT | Safari Books Online

Learning Swift™ Programming

Jacob Schatz

✦ Addison-Wesley

Upper Saddle River, NJ • Boston • Indianapolis • San Francisco
New York • Toronto • Montreal • London • Munich • Paris • Madrid
Cape Town • Sydney • Tokyo • Singapore • Mexico City

Learning Swift™ Programming

Copyright © 2015 by Pearson Education, Inc.

ISBN-13: 978-0-13-395040-3

ISBN-10: 0-13-395040-9

Library of Congress Control Number: 2014956093

Printed in the United States of America

First Printing: December 2014

Trademarks

All terms mentioned in this book that are known to be trademarks or service marks have been appropriately capitalized. The publisher cannot attest to the accuracy of this information. Use of a term in this book should not be regarded as affecting the validity of any trademark or service mark.

Warning and Disclaimer

Every effort has been made to make this book as complete and as accurate as possible, but no warranty or fitness is implied. The information provided is on an "as is" basis. The author and the publisher shall have neither liability nor responsibility to any person or entity with respect to any loss or damages arising from the information contained in this book.

Special Sales

For information about buying this title in bulk quantities, or for special sales opportunities (which may include electronic versions; custom cover designs; and content particular to your business, training goals, marketing focus, or branding interests), please contact our corporate sales department at corpsales@pearsoned.com or (800) 382-3419.

For government sales inquiries, please contact governmentsales@pearsoned.com.

For questions about sales outside the U.S., please contact international@pearsoned.com.

Acquisitions Editor
Mark Taber

Managing Editor
Sandra Schroeder

Project Editor
Mandie Frank

Copy Editor
Kitty Wilson

Indexer
Cheryl Lenser

Proofreader
Paula Lowell

Technical Editor
Mike Keen

Editorial Assistant
Vanessa Evans

Designer
Chuti Prasertsith

Compositor
Mary Sudul

❖

For Tiffany and Noa

❖

Contents at a Glance

Table of Contents

About the Author

Jacob Schatz is a senior software engineer with more than eight years of experience writing code for the masses. His popular Skip Wilson YouTube channel has helped thousands of people around the world learn programming languages like Swift and Python. Though lately he has been deep into Swift, he also writes volumes of code in JavaScript, Python, Objective-C, and other languages. Jacob is always selectively consuming the latest programming trends. He has a passion for making a difference and is constantly solving problems. Lately he has been deep into Swift; he also writes volumes of code in JavaScript, Python, Objective-C, and other languages. He is always learning additional languages and thoroughly enjoys making new things. He is, at heart, an educator, and enjoys teaching and finding new ways to explain advanced concepts.

Acknowledgments

I could not have written this book without the help of many people. Thank you to the following:

Logan Wright, who wrote tons of YouTube tutorials with me and helped me with this book.

Cody Romano, who graciously helped me write and proofread, and whose endless knowledge has helped me debug more than a few bugs.

Mike Keen, who tirelessly proofread chapters and tried all my examples to make sure they were legit. He also provided an endless source of inspiration.

Mom and Dad, who, even though they had no idea what they were reading, sat there and read this book thoroughly, providing sage advice.

My wife, who put up with me spending countless hours in front of my computer, and through the process of this book has become an advanced programmer.

We Want to Hear from You!

As the reader of this book, you are our most important critic and commentator. We value your opinion and want to know what we're doing right, what we could do better, what areas you'd like to see us publish in, and any other words of wisdom you're willing to pass our way.

We welcome your comments. You can email or write directly to let us know what you did or didn't like about this book—as well as what we can do to make our books better.

Please note that we cannot help you with technical problems related to the topic of this book, and that due to the high volume of mail we receive, we might not be able to reply to every message.

When you write, please be sure to include this book's title and author, as well as your name and phone or email address.

Email: feedback@developers-library.info

Mail: Reader Feedback
          Addison-Wesley Developer's Library
          800 East 96th Street
          Indianapolis, IN 46240 USA

Reader Services

Visit our website and register this book at **www.informit.com/register** for convenient access to any updates, downloads, or errata that might be available for this book.

Introduction

Welcome to Learning Swift Programming. *This book will launch you into the world of iOS programming using the exciting new Swift programming language. This book covers the Swift programming language from start to finish, in a quick but complete way.*

This introduction covers:

- *Who should read this book*

- *Why you should read this book*

- *What you will be able to achieve using this book*

- *What Swift is and why it is awesome*

- *How this book is organized*

- *Where to find the code examples*

Ready?

Who Should Read This Book

This book is for those who already have one or many programming languages under their belt. You may be able to get through this book with Swift as your first language, but you'll find it easier if you can relate it to other languages. If you have experience with iOS programming with Objective-C, then you should really be able to take to Swift quickly. This book often relates Swift concepts to those of other popular programming languages, including JavaScript, Python, Ruby, C, and Objective-C.

Why You Should Read This Book

This book will teach you all aspects of Swift programming so you can start writing high-quality apps as quickly as possible. However, it is not an exhaustive reference; it is a complete yet easy-to-digest initiation into Swift. This book will make you a better developer; because Swift is a mixture of many different languages you are bound to learn new concepts here. Swift is very robust on its own and at the same time it allows you to mix in Objective-C.

If you are reading this book, you''ve probably heard people talking about Swift's amazing features. You''ve heard about its advanced design, how fast it runs, and how much easier your development will be. This book shows you all those features of the Swift language, as well as some very exciting discoveries I've made with it. You will be part of a revolution, as you will be one of the first Swift programmers in the world. Swift has been around only a couple months, but expect it to be around for a very long time. Now is the perfect time to jump right in. This book will get you fully immersed and provide everything you need to get up and running as quickly as possible.

What You Will Learn from This Book

Reading this book will make you an official Swift programmer and allow you to write real-world, production-quality apps. You'll write apps that take advantage of the most advanced features of Swift, so you'll be writing refined, clean code. After reading this book, you'll be able to create any app you want in Swift. Here are just a few things you will learn while reading this book:

- How to combine existing Objective-C code into new Swift applications
- How to use advanced features like generics to write less code
- How to create optionals as a quicker way to make sure your code doesn't crash at runtime due to nonexistent values
- How to write closures to pass around little blocks of functionality, which can be written in as little as four characters
- How to create a 2D side-scrolling game using SpriteKit
- How to create a 3D game using SceneKit
- How to read bits and bytes so you can do things like read a PDF

What Is Swift?

Swift is a new programming language from Apple that replaces and also works alongside languages like C and Objective-C. The idea with Swift is to make it easier to write apps for iOS with a language that is fresh and new. The Swift language relates to many other languages. It is also so customizable that you can write Swift in many different ways. For example, Swift allows you to define what square brackets do; instead of always using them for array and dictionary access, you can technically make them do whatever you want. Swift allows you to define your own operators and override existing ones. If you want to make a new triple incrementor (such as +++) that increments twice instead of once, then you can do that. Plus, you can create custom operators to work with your custom classes, which means you'll write less code and therefore make your life easier. For example, if you were to write a program about automobiles, you could define what would happen if you were to add two cars instances to each other. Normally you can only add numbers to each other, but in Swift you can override the + operator to do whatever you want.

Swift is well structured and completely compatible with Objective-C. All the libraries available in Objective-C are also available in Swift. Swift allows you to create bridges that connect languages.

How This Book Is Organized

This book is divided into 12 chapters, which cover the language itself and walk you through creating a few apps:

- Chapters 1–4 cover basic language syntax, including variables, constants, arrays, dictionaries, functions, classes, enums, and structs. These are the basic building blocks of the Swift language.

- Chapter 5 takes a break from the language syntax and helps you create a basic game of tic-tac-toe.

- Chapters 6–9 cover more advanced language features, including closures, subscripts, advanced operators, protocols and extensions, generics, and programming on the bit and byte levels.

- Chapters 10–12 show you how to create real-world apps using the knowledge you've gained from previous chapters.

Enjoy the Ride

My goal was to make this book fun to read, and I had a lot of fun writing it. I want to show you how exciting learning a new language can be.

When a new language comes out, often not a whole lot of knowledge is out there about it. This book aims to give you direct access to knowledge that is hard to find, and it is an easy-to-read version of a lot of knowledge that is hard to read. Searching online for answers can be difficult as Swift evolves and we all are still figuring out Swift together. There are, of course, bugs in the language, and I'm sure there will continue to be bugs. I wrote this book while Swift was still in beta (and constantly changing) and finished it up as Swift became version 1.0. Swift will continue to change and improve the more people use it and report bugs as time goes on. This book has been tested against the latest version of Swift (as of this writing), but that doesn't mean that Swift won't change. I hope you enjoy learning to use Swift.

1

Getting Your Feet Wet

Swift was released in 2014, but its development started four years earlier. Chris Lattner, the original author of the LLVM compiler and the director of Apple's Developer Tools Department, has worked for Apple since 2005. He had to develop Swift in secret for several years and was, amazingly, able to keep it under wraps until its release in June 2014.

This chapter covers the basic building blocks of Swift. It starts with variables and constants, which allow you to reference a storage location by name. With this knowledge, you will be able to store stuff in memory. Swift has a special feature called optionals, *which allow you to check for the presence of a value (by determining whether the variable or constant is* nil*). Swift has strong type inference; this allows you to have strict typing without needing to declare a type. This chapter reviews how Swift handles loops and* if/else *statements.*

Building Blocks of Swift

Swift allows you to use variables and constants by associating a name with a value of some type. For example, if you want to store the string "Hi" in a variable named greeting, you can use a variable or a constant. You create a variable by using the var keyword. This establishes an associated value that can be changed during the execution of the program. If you do not want that value to be changed, you can use a constant. For example, you might record the number of login retries a user is allowed to have before being refused access to the site. In such a case, you would want to use a constant, as shown in this example:

```
let numberOfRetries = 5
var currentRetries = 0
```

Notice that you don't use a semicolon as you would in many other languages. You do not need to use semicolons to denote the end of a statement unless you want to combine many statements together. Swift is very different from JavaScript, where omitting semicolons is generally considered unsafe. This example shows you when you would use the semicolon in Swift as multiple lines are combined into one:

```
let numberOfRetries = 5; var currentRetries = 0
```

Also unique to Swift, you can use almost any Unicode character to name your variables and constants. Developers can name resources using Hebrew, Simplified Chinese, and even special Unicode characters, such as full-color koala emoji (which is a unique Apple invention).

Using Comments

You indicate comments in Swift by using a double forward slash, exactly as in Objective-C. Here's an example:

```
// This is a comment about the number of retries
let numberOfRetries = 5 // We can also put a comment on the end of a line.
/* Comments can span
multiple lines */
```

Inference Everywhere!

Swift uses inference to figure out what *types* you are attempting to use. Because of this, you do not need to declare a type when creating variables and constants. However, if you want to declare a type you may do so, and in certain situations, it is absolutely necessary. When declaring a variable, the rule of thumb is that Swift needs to know what type it is. If Swift cannot figure out the type, you need to be more explicit. The following is a valid statement:

```
var currentRetries = 0
```

Notice that Swift has to figure out what type of number this is. currentRetries may be one of the many types of numbers that Swift offers (Swift will infer this as an Int in case you are wondering, but more on that later). You could also use this:

```
var currentRetries:Int = 0
```

In this case, you explicitly set the type to Int by using the colon after the variable name to declare a type. While this is legit, it is unnecessary because Swift already knows that 0 is an Int. Swift will infer a type with initial values.

You need to declare the type if you do not know what the initial value of currentRetries will be. For example:

```
var currentRetries:Int
```

In this case, you must declare Int because without it, Swift cannot tell what type this variable will be. This is called *type safety*. If Swift expects a string, you must pass it a string. You cannot pass an Int when a String is expected. This is a great time saver because it means you do a lot less typing (with your fingers). Swift does a lot of the typing (inference) for you. Thanks, Swift! Swift is completely compatible with Objective-C and is able to use almost all of the APIs available to Objective-C and C (if not you can make your own bridge to make the API available). Swift also has its own types separate from Objective-C and C. For number types, Swift gives us the following:

- Int provides 8-, 16-, 32-, and 64-bit flavors, but you will most likely stay with just Int. It's probably large enough for your needs. Here's what you need to know about Int:

  Int on 32-bit platforms is Int32.

  Int on 64-bit platforms is Int64.

  That is, when you declare a variable as Int, Swift will do the work of changing that to Int32 or Int64. You don't need to do anything on your end.

  Int can be both positive and negative in value.

  Int will be chosen when you declare a variable with an integer:

  ```
  var someInt = 3 // this will be an Int
  ```

  UInt is provided as an *unsigned* integer. An unsigned number must be greater than or equal to zero, whereas a *signed* number can be negative. For consistency, Apple recommends that you generally use Int even when you know a value will never be negative.

- Double denotes 64-bit floating-point numbers. Double has a higher precision than float, with at least 15 decimal digits. Double will be chosen when you declare a variable with a floating-point number:

  ```
  var someDouble = 3.14 // this will be a double
  ```

  Combining any integer with any floating-point number results in a Double:

  ```
  3 + 3.14 // 6.14 Works and will be a double
  var three = 3
  var threePointOne = 3.1
  three + threePointOne //Error because you can't mix types
  ```

- Float denotes 32-bit floating-point numbers. Float can have a precision as small as 6. Whether you choose Float or Double is completely up to you and your situation. Swift will choose Double when no type is declared.

Along with Decimal numbers, you can use Binary, Octal, and Hexadecimal numbers:

- Decimal is the default for all numbers, so no prefix is needed.
- Binary takes a 0b prefix.
- Octal takes a 0o prefix.
- Hexadecimal takes a 0x prefix.

You can check the type of the object like this:

```
var pi:Any?
pi = 3.141
pi is Double //true
pi is Float  //false
```

You can test the class or type of an object (introspect) in this way. Notice how you declare this type as `Any?` in the preceding example. (You will learn more about `Any` in more detail later.) The question mark means that you want an optional (and you'll learn more about this shortly as well). The `Any` type can be any type (exactly what it says). Because Objective-C is not as strict as Swift, and you need to be able to intermingle the two languages, `Any` and `AnyObject` were created. You'll learn more about this later in the chapter.

Swift is one of the few programming languages that let you put underscores in numbers to make them more legible. Xcode ignores the underscores when it evaluates your code. You might find using underscores especially useful with big numbers, where you want to denote the thousand-comma separator, as in this case:

```
var twoMil = 2_000_000
```

Before you can add two numbers together, they must be of the same type. For example, the following will not work:

```
var someNumA:UInt8 = 8
var someNumB:Int8 = 9
someNumA + someNumB
//Int8 is not convertible to UInt8
```

In order to make this work, you must convert one of the types to the other by using the *initializer*. For example, you can use the initializer `UInt8`, which can convert for you:

```
someNumA + UInt8(someNumB)
```

Swift is strict in requiring you to convert types before you can combine them.

Optionals: A Gift to Unwrap

Optionals are a unique feature of Swift, and they are used absolutely everywhere. Optionals take a little getting used to but in the end they are a clever feature that helps you achieve clean-looking code with fewer lines while also being stricter.

In many languages, you need to check objects to see whether they are `nil` or `null`. Usually, you write some pseudo-code that looks like the following. In this example we check for not null in Javascript:

```
if(something != null) {...
```

Not having to write that ugly code all over the place saves you time. In Swift, an optional value contains either a value or `nil` to indicate that the value is missing. To mark something as optional, you just include a ? next to the type of the object. For example, here's how you create a String optional:

```
var someString:String? = "Hey there!"
```

You can now say that someString is of type String? (which you verbalize as "String optional") and not just of type String. Try printing that variable as an optional string and then as a regular string. Notice the difference in their returned values.

What makes optionals unique is that they must be "unwrapped" in order to get their value back. There are a couple ways to get the value out of an optional. When you see a variable of type String?, you can say that this variable may or may not contain a value. You can say, "I will test this String optional to find out if it does in fact have a value." How do you test an optional? You use *value binding*.

Value binding allows you to do two things at once. First, it allows you to test the optional to see whether it is nil. Second, if that variable is not nil, value binding allows you to grab the value out of the optional and have it passed into a constant as a locally scoped variable. To see this in action, you'll look at an example, but before you can try it out, you first need to open a new playground:

1. Open Xcode 6.

2. Click Get started with a playground.

3. Save a new playground file by giving it a filename.

Now you can try out value binding with optionals:

```
var hasSomething:String? = "Hey there!"
if let message = hasSomething {
    "Message was legit: \(message)"
} else {
    "There was no message!"
}
```

A couple of fancy new things are going on here. This short little blurb of code is one of the things that make Swift so fantastic. Let's go through it one step at a time:

1. On the first line, you create a variable as usual, but you add the ? to say that this is a String optional. This means that this String may contain a value or nil. In this case, it contains a value.

2. Next, you write a conditional statement. You are testing whether the variable hasSomething is nil or not. At the same time, you are assigning that value of the optional to a constant message. If the variable contains a value, then you get a new constant (only available in the local scope, so we call it a locally scope constant), which is populated with the raw value of the optional. You will then enter into the if statement body.

3. If you do enter into that `if` statement, you now have a locally scoped constant `message` to use. This constant will not be available anywhere else in the code. You can then print a string, which contains the locally scoped constant. Swift has a special syntax for including variables in strings without having to concatenate strings in the old-school way. You can write `\()` and include the variable inside those parentheses. Doing this prints the variable's contents in the middle of the string. In other languages, you might have to do something like this. Here is an example of what you might do in JavaScript on the first line and then in Objective-C on the second line:

```
"Message was legit" + message;
[NSString stringWithFormat:@"Message was legit: %@", message];
```

However, sometimes, you are absolutely sure that your optional contains a value. Swift uses optionals here. (We will get into arrays and dictionaries in Chapter 2, but think about it: If you try to grab an item from a dictionary, that item may or may not exist.) You can think of optionals as a gift that needs to be unwrapped. Now if this optional is `nil` inside, it will not throw an error when you try to access it, because you haven't unwrapped it. In most languages, trying to access something of `nil` value throws an error. In the case of the dictionary, sometimes you are sure that the dictionary item has a value. You want to *implicitly unwrap* the optional.

You can force the unwrapping of an optional to get that value out by using an exclamation point. Let's look again at our earlier example. If you were sure that the string contained a value, you could force an unwrapping of the optional like this (try it out in a playground):

```
var hasSomething:String? = "Hey there!" //declare the optional string
hasSomething // prints {Some "Hey there!"}
//Now force the optional to unwrap with !
hasSomething! // prints "Hey there!"
```

Now you can get the value out of the optional with one extra character. Remember how we said these optionals are like presents? Well, it's sometimes good to think of them more like bombs in Minesweeper. If you are too young for Minesweeper, then think of them as presents that could contain bombs. You want to force the unwrapping of an optional only if you are sure its value is not `nil`. If you force the unwrapping of an optional that does contain `nil`, then you will throw a fatal error, and your program will crash:

```
var hasSomething:String? //declare the optional string with no initial
    value
// Now try and force it open
hasSomething! // fatal error: unexpectedly found nil while unwrapping an Optional
value your program will crash and probably won't be accepted to the app store.
```

You want to get the output of the code so open up the console of the playground so you can see your output. Click the little circle in the output area or by pressing Command+Alt+Enter.

Printing Your Results

When you use the playground to test your code, you have two options for printing data. You can simply just write it, like this:

```
var someString = "hi there"
someString //prints "hi there" in the output area
```

You can also use `println()`, which prints to the console output area. When you are making a full-fledged app, compiling code outside a playground, you'll want to use `println()`, like this, because just writing the variable will not do anything:

```
var someString = "hi there"
println(someString) //prints "hi there" in the console output
```

Implicitly Unwrapped Optionals

Sometimes you want to create an optional that gets unwrapped automatically. To do this, you assign the type with an exclamation point instead of a question mark:

```
var hasSomething:String! = "Hey there"// implicitly unwrapped optional string
hasSomething // print the implicitly unwrapped optional and get the
    unwrapped value.
```

You can think of implicitly unwrapped optionals as a present that unwraps itself. You should not use an implicitly unwrapped optional if a chance exists that it may contain `nil` at any point. You can still use implicitly unwrapped optionals in value binding to check their values.

So why should you create implicitly unwrapped optionals in the first place if they can be automatically unwrapped? How does that make them any better than regular variables? Why even use them in the first place? These are fantastic questions, and we will answer them later, after we talk about classes and structures in Chapter 4. One quick answer is that sometimes we want to say that something has no value initially but we promise that it will have a value later. Properties of classes must be given a value by the time initialization is complete. We can declare a property with the exclamation point to say "Right now it does not have a value, but we promise we will give this property a value at some point."

Tuples

Using *tuples* (pronounced "TWO-pulls" or "TUH-pulls") is a way to group multiple values into one. Think of associated values. Here is an example with URL settings:

```
let purchaseEndpoint = ("buy","POST","/buy/")
```

This tuple has a `String`, a `String`, and a `String`. This tuple is considered to be of type (`String`, `String`, `String`). You can put as many values as you want in a tuple, but you should use them for what they are meant for. You can mix types in tuples as well, like this:

```
let purchaseEndpoint = ("buy","POST","/buy/",true)
```

This tuple has a `String`, a `String`, a `String`, and a `Bool`. You are mixing types here, and this tuple is considered to be of type (`String`, `String`, `String`, `Bool`). You can access this tuple by using its indexes:

```
purchaseEndpoint.1 // "POST"
purchaseEndpoint.2 // "/buy/"
```

There are two problems here. You can guess what `POST` and `/buy/` are, but what does `true` stand for? Also, using indexes to access the tuple is not very pretty or descriptive. You need to be able to be more expressive with the tuple.

You can take advantage of Swift's ability to name individual elements to make your intentions clearer:

```
let purchaseEndpoint = (name: "buy", httpMethod: "POST",URL:
"/buy/",useAuth: true)
```

This tuple has `String`, `String`, `String`, and `Bool` (true or false) values. Now you can access the elements in a much prettier way:

```
purchaseEndpoint.httpMethod = "POST"
```

Now this is much better. It makes much more sense and reads more like English.

You can *decompose* this tuple into multiple variables at once, like so:

```
let (purchaseName, purchaseMethod, purchaseURL, _) = purchaseEndpoint
```

Here, you are able to take three variables and grab the meat out of the tuple and assign it right to those variables. You use an underscore to say that you don't need the fourth element out of the tuple.

In Chapter 3, "Making Things Happen: Functions," you will use tuples to give functions multiple return values. You can probably imagine how this would work. Imagine having a function that returned a tuple instead of a string. You could then return all the data at once and do something like this:

```
let purchaseEndpoint = getEndpoint("buy") // some function that doesn't exist yet
println("You can access the purchase url at \(purchaseEndpoint.URL) using a
    \(purchaseEndpoint.httpMethod)")
```

Number Types and Converting Between Them

Swift is interoperable with Objective-C, so you can use C, Objective-C, and Swift types all within Swift. As discussed earlier in the chapter, when you write a variable using an integer, Swift automatically declares it with a type `Int`, without your having to tell Swift you want an `Int`. In this example, you don't tell Swift to make this variable an `Int`:

```
let theAnswerToLifeTheUniverseAndEverything = 42
```

Rather, Swift infers that it is an `Int`. Remember that on 32-bit systems, this `Int` will be an `Int32` and on 64-bit systems, it will be an `Int64`. Even though you have many different `Int` types available to you, unless you have a need for an `Int` of a specific size, you should stick with Swift's `Int`. When we say `Int32`, what we mean is a 32-bit integer. (This is similar to C.) You can also use `UInt` for unsigned (non-negative) integers, but Apple recommends that you stick with `Int` even if you know your variable is going to be unsigned.

Again, when you write any type of floating-point number (a number with a decimal), and you don't assign a type, Swift automatically declares it with the type `Double`. Swift gives you `Double` and `Float` types. The difference between them is that `Double` has a higher precision of around 15 decimal digits, whereas `Float` has around 6. You have to decide at coding time which is right for your situation. Here is an example of Swift automatically converting to a `Double`:

```
let gamma = 0.5772156649015328606065120900824024310421593359392
gamma //prints 0.577215664901533 which is 15 decimal places. Inferred to a
    double
```

Swift is strict about its types and how you can combine them together. If something is meant to be a `String`, and you give it an `Int`, then you will get an error. Swift wants you to be explicit with types. For example, this will not work:

```
var someInt = 5 // Inferred to be an Int
someInt + 3.141 // throws an error
```

If you want to combine an `Int` and a `Double` you must first convert the `Int` to a `Double` or vice versa, depending on your preference. Here we combine an `Int` and `Double` by converting the `Int` to a `Double`:

```
var someInt = 5 // Inferred to be an Int
Double(someInt) + 3.141
```

```
var someInt = 5 // Inferred to be an Int
Float(someInt) + 3.141 // In this case 3.141 will be inferred to a Float so
    it can combine with a Float
```

```
var someInt = 5 // Inferred to be an Int
Float(someInt) + Double(3.141) //This will throw an error and will not work
```

You can use the initializer of the number type to convert between types. For example, you can use `Float()` to convert any number type into a `Float`. You can see why this works if you look in the source code by holding Command and clicking the word `Float`. You then now see the `Float` source (in summary, not the real deal). If you go down to around line 2096, you see that Swift has created initializers for every other number type. It uses extensions to achieve this. You can probably guess that Swift takes the `Float` source and *extends* it with new initializers and other functionality. What is so cool about this is that you can do the same thing yourself. Apple wrote Swift with Swift.

So again, when you want to perform any operations on two or more number types, all sides of the operation must be of the same type. You'll see this pattern often in Swift, and not just with numbers. For example, you cannot directly add a `UInt8` and a `UInt16` unless you first convert the `UInt8` to a `UInt16` or vice versa.

Coming to Swift from Objective-C and C

If you are coming from a world of Objective-C and C, then you know that you have many number types at your disposal. Number types like `CGFloat` and `CFloat` are necessary to construct certain objects. For example, SpriteKit has the `SKSpriteNode` as a position property, which is a `CGPoint` with two `CGFloats`.

What do you do? What is the different between `CGFloat` and `Float`? Well if you Command+click the `CGFloat`, you see that `CGFloat` is just a `typealias` for `Double`. This is what the code actually says:

```
typealias CGFloat = Double
```

What is a `typealias`? Great question. A `typealias` is just a shortcut name to an already existing type. It basically gives the type a substitute name. You could give `String` an alternate name type of `Text`, like this:

```
typealias Text = String
var hello:Text = "Hi there"
```

Now `hello` is of type `Text`, which was previously nonexistent. So if `CGFloat` is a `typealias` for a `Double`, this just means that when you make `CGFloats`, you are really just making `Doubles`. It's worth it to Command+click around and see what is mapping to what. For example, a `CFloat` is a `typealias` for `Float`, and a `CDouble` is a `typealias` for `Double`.

Control Flow: Making Choices

Controlling the order in which code executes is a crucial aspect of any programming language. By building on the traditions of C and C-like languages, Swift's control flow constructs allow for powerful functionality while still maintaining a familiar syntax.

`for` Loops

At its most basic, a `for` loop allows you to execute code repeatedly. You can also say that code statements are "looping" a certain number of times (or infinitely). In the Swift language, there are two distinct types of `for` loops to consider. There is the traditional `for-condition-increment` loop, and there is the `for-in` loop. `for-in` is often associated with a process known as *fast enumeration*—a simplified syntax that makes it easier to run specific code for every item in a range, sequence, collection, or progression. Using `for-in` also decreases the implementation overhead.

`for-condition-increment` Loops

You use a `for-condition-increment` loop to run code repeatedly until a condition is met. On each loop, you typically increment a counter until the counter reaches the desired value. You can also decrement the counter until it drops to a certain value, but that is less common. The basic syntax of this type of loop in Swift looks something like this:

```
for initialization; conditional expression; increment {
    statement
}
```

As in Objective-C and C, in Swift you use semicolons to separate the different components of the `for` loop. However, Swift doesn't group these components into parentheses. Aside from this slight syntactic difference, `for` loops in Swift function as they would in any C language.

Here's a simple example of a `for-condition-increment` loop that simply prints `Hello` a few times.

```
for var i = 0; i < 5; ++i {
    println("Hello there number \(i)")
}
// Hello there number 0
// Hello there number 1
// Hello there number 2
// Hello there number 3
// Hello there number 4
```

This is fairly straightforward, but notice the following:

- Variables or constants declared in the *initialization expression* are valid only within the scope of the loop itself. If you need to access these values outside the scope of the `for` loop, then the variable must be declared prior to entering the loop, like this:

```
        var i = 0
for i; i < 5; ++i {...
```

- If you're coming from another language, particularly Objective-C, you will notice that the preceding example uses `++i` instead of `i++`. Using `++i` increments `i` before returning its value, while `i++` increments `i` after returning its value. Although this won't make much of a difference in the earlier example, Apple specifically suggests that you use the `++i` implementation unless the behavior of `i++` is explicitly necessary.

- To avoid an infinite loop, it is necessary to create a `for` loop where the *conditional expression* will eventually evaluate to `false`. The earlier example increments `i` after each time the bracketed statements execute, and the *conditional expression* (`i < 5`) will be false when `i` is 5 or greater; at that point, the loop exits. Writing `true` in there would make it loop forever.

for-in Loops

In addition to giving you the traditional for-condition-increment loop, Swift builds on the enumeration concepts of Objective-C and provides an extremely powerful for-in statement. Its syntax makes some of the most common use cases extremely concise and easy.

With for-in, you can iterate numbers in a range. For example, you could use a for-in loop to calculate values over time. Here you can loop through 1 to 4 with less typing:

```
class Tire { }
var tires = [Tire]()
for i in 1...4 {
    tires.append(Tire())
}
println("We have \(tires.count))
```

You can ignore the class and array syntax here since we haven't covered it yet. This example uses a ... range operator for an inclusive range. This means that the range begins at the first number and includes all the numbers up to and including the second number. If you wanted to go up to the second number but not include it, you would use the ..< range operator. The previous example, rewritten to use the non-inclusive range operator, would look like this:

```
class Tire { }
var tires = [Tire]()
// 1,2,3 but not 4
for i in 1..<4 {
    tires.append(Tire())
}
println("We have \(tires.count))
```

As you can see, the results are almost identical, and whichever form you choose is largely a matter of what you need. Both examples provide concise and readable code. In situations where you don't need access to i, you can disregard the variable altogether by replacing it with an underscore (_). The code now might look something like this:

```
class Tire { }
var tires = [Tire]()
// 1,2,3, and including 4
for _ in 1...4 {
    tires.append(Tire())
}
println("We have \(tires.count))
```

Another extremely common use of for loops is to iterate through collections and perform a set of statements for each item within the collection. Let's pretend that a bunch of tires have gone flat, and you need to refill them with air. You could use this Swift code:

```
class Tire {var air = 0}
for tire in tires {
    tire.air = 100
}
```

With this type of declaration, Swift uses *type inference* to assume that each object in an array of type [Tire] will be a Tire. This means it is unnecessary to declare the type explicitly. In a situation where the array's type is unknown, the implementation would look like this:

```
class Tire {var air = 0}
for tire: Tire in tires {
    tire.air = 100
}
println("We made \(tires.count) tires")
// We made 4 tires
```

Swift always has to know the type.

In Swift, a String is really a collection of Character values in a specific order. You can iterate values in a String by using a for-in statement, like so:

```
for char in "abcdefghijklmnopqrstuvwxyz" {
    println(char)
}
// a
// b
// c
// etc ...
```

As with any other collection, it is simple and concise to iterate through each item. There are still situations in which you need access to the index number as well as the object. One option is to iterate through a range of indexes and then get the object at the index. You would write that like this:

```
let array = ["zero", "one", "two", "three", "four"]
for idx in 0..<array.count {
    let numberString = array[idx]
    println("Number at index \(idx) is \(numberString)")
}
// Number at index 0 is zero
// Number at index 1 is one
// etc ...
```

This code executes fine, but Swift provides a global enumerate function that makes this type of statement a bit more concise. If you were to use the for-in statement in conjunction with the enumerate function, the preceding example would look like this:

```
let array = ["zero", "one", "two", "three", "four"]
for (idx, numberString) in enumerate(array) {
    println("Number at index \(idx) is \(numberString)")
}
// Number at index 0 is zero
// Number at index 1 is one
// etc ...
```

This type of enumeration is extremely clear and concise, and you would use it when the situation requires an array element and its index. You are able to grab the index of the loop and the item being iterated over!

Up to this point, all the code in this chapter has known ahead of time how many times it should iterate. For situations in which the number of required iterations is unknown, it can be useful to use a while loop or a do while loop. The syntax to use these while loops is very similar to that in other languages, minus the parentheses. Here's an example:

```
var i = 0
while i < 10 {
    i++
}
```

Here, you are saying that this loop should continue while the value of i is less than 10. In this situation, i starts out at 0, and on each run of the loop, i gets incremented by 1. You can have an infinite loop this way. You have to decide if you need an infinite loop. There are times when an infinite loop is necessary.

For example, in the playground, some types of code won't respond to a URL callback because the NSRunLoop isn't running. For instance, trying to grab some data from a URL with NSSession.sharedSession().dataTaskWithURL() does not work because the NSRunLoop is listening for things like URL callbacks. You need to do a little hack to get the run loop running: use a continuous while loop that never ends. In this case, you'll use while true to achieve this:

```
import Cocoa
import XCPlayground
while true {
    NSRunLoop.currentRunLoop().runMode(
            NSDefaultRunLoopMode,
            beforeDate:NSDate()
    )
    usleep(10)
}
```

Now things like dataTaskWithURL will work in the playground. Notice in this example you use a while loop that always evaluates to true. Therefore, this loop will loop forever.

The following example combines all the looping capabilities and if/else statements you now know about to find the prime numbers. Here's how you could find the 200th prime number:

```
import Cocoa
var primeList = [2.0]
var num = 3.0
var isPrime = 1
while countElements(primeList) < 200 {
    var sqrtNum = sqrt(num)
    // test by dividing only with prime numbers
```

```
    for primeNumber in primeList {
        // skip testing with prime numbers greater
        // than square root of number
        if num % primeNumber == 0 {
            isPrime = 0
            break
        }
        if primeNumber > sqrtNum {
            break
        }
    }
    if isPrime == 1 {
        primeList.append(num)
    } else {
        isPrime = 1
    }
    //skip even numbers
    num += 2
}
primeList[199]
```

Grabbing `primeList[199]` will grab the 200th prime number because arrays start at 0. You can combine `while` loops with `for-in` loops to calculate prime numbers. If you try this out in the playground, make sure that your `while` loop does not run while you are writing your code, or you might get super annoyed because the `while` loop will go on forever while you try to type, and this may crash your Xcode. Try setting `while` to `false`. Then change it back when you are done.

Making Choices with Conditionals (if/else)

It's important to be able to make your code make decisions and change directions. Without this, your code would take the same path every time it is run. You make if/else choices yourself all the time. You might say to yourself, "I'll keep pouring water in this glass *if* the water is below the top line of the glass." Or you might say to yourself, "*If* the car in front of me slows down below 55 mph, I'll pass him on the left. Otherwise, I'll stay in this lane." Your decision making is more complicated than this, though. You need to think of other factors and might say something like, "*If* the driver in front of me slows down below 55 mph, I'll pass him on the left *if* no one in the third lane is coming *and if* there are no cops around." Here's how you might make such decision making in Swift code:

```
var carInFrontSpeed = 54
if carInFrontSpeed < 55 {
    println("I am passing on the left")
} else {
    println("I will stay in this lane")
}
```

Here, you use Swift's `if` and `else` statements to make a decision based on whether a variable is less than 55. Since the integer 54 is less than the integer 55, you show the statement in the `if` section. One caveat to `if` statements is that they cannot use integers converted to `true` or `false`. For example, the following will throw an error.

```
if 1 { //throws an error
    //Do something
}
```

In the highway passing example, you want to check multiple statements to see if they're `true` or `false`. You want to check whether the car in front of you slows down below 55 mph and whether there is a car coming and whether there is a police car nearby. You can check all three in one statement with the `&&` operator to say that the statement to the left of the `&&` must be true as well as the statement to the right of the `&&`. Here's what it looks like:

```
var policeNearBy = false
var carInLane3 = false
var carInFrontSpeed = 45
if !policeNearBy && !carInLane3 && carInFrontSpeed < 55 {
    println("We are going to pass the car.")
} else {
    println("We will stay right where we are for now.")
}
```

In this example, you make sure that all three situations are `false` before you move into the next lane. You can also check to see if any of the statements are `true` by using the or operator, which is written as two pipes: `||`. You could rewrite the preceding statement by using the or operator. This example just checks for the opposite of what the last example checks for:

```
var policeNearBy = false
var carInLane3 = false
var carInFrontSpeed = 45
if policeNearBy || carInLane3 || carInFrontSpeed > 55 {
    println("We will stay right where we are for now.")
} else {
    println("We are going to pass the car.")
}
```

If any of the preceding variables are `true`, then you will stay where you are: You will not pass the car.

Sometimes you need to check for other conditions. You might want to check whether one condition is not met instead of just going straight to an `else`. You can use `else if` for this purpose, as shown in this example:

```
var policeNearBy = false
var carInLane3 = false
var carInFrontSpeed = 45
var backSeatDriverIsComplaining = true
```

```
if policeNearBy || carInLane3 || carInFrontSpeed > 55 {
    println("We will stay right where we are for now.")
} else if backSeatDriverIsComplaining {
    println("We will try to pass in a few minutes")
}else {
    println("We are going to pass the car.")
}
```

You can group as many of these else ifs together as you need. However, when you start grouping a bunch of else if statements together, it might be time to use the switch statement.

Switching It Up: switch Statements

You get much more control if you use a switch statement to control your flow instead of using tons of if else statements. Swift's switch statements are very similar to those in other languages with some extra power added in. One little caveat is that in Swift, you do not have to use break to stop a condition from running through each case statement. Swift automatically breaks on its own when the condition is met.

Another caveat about switch statements is that they must be exhaustive. That is, if you are using a switch statement on an int, then you need to provide a case for every int *ever*. Because this is not possible, you can use the default statement to provide a match when nothing else matches. Here is a basic switch statement:

```
var num = 5
switch num {
case 2:println("It's two")
case 3:println("It's three")
default:println("It's something else")
}
```

Notice that you must add a default statement. As mentioned earlier, if you try removing it, you will get an error because the switch statement must exhaust every possibility. Also note that case 3 will not run if case 2 is matched because Swift automatically breaks for you.

You can also check multiple values at once. This is similar to using the or operator (||) in if else statements. Here's how you do it:

```
var num = 5
switch num {
case 2,3,4:println("It's two") // is it 2 or 3 or 4?
case 5,6:println("it's five") // is it 5 or 6?
default:println("It's something else")
}
```

In addition, you can check ranges. The following example determines whether a number is something between 2 and 6:

```
var num = 5
switch num {
// including 2,3,4,5,6
case 2...6:println("num is between 2 to 6")
default:println("None of the above")
}
```

You can use tuples in `switch` statements. You can use the underscore character (_) to tell Swift to "match everything." You can also check for ranges in tuples. Here's how you could match a geographic location:

```
var geo = (2,4)
switch geo {
//(anything, 5)
case (_,5):println("It's (Something,5)")
case (5,_):println("It's (5,Something)")
case (1...3,_):println("It's (1 2 or 3, Something)")
case (1...3,3...6):println("This would have matched but Swift already found
    a match")
default:println("It's something else")
}
```

In the first `case`, you are first trying to find a tuple whose first number is anything and whose second number is 5.

In the second `case`, you are looking for the opposite of the first `case`.

In the third `case`, you are looking for any number in the range 1 to 3, including 3, and the second number can be anything. Matching this `case` causes the `switch` to exit.

The next `case` would also match, but Swift has already found a match, so it never executes.

If you want the typical Objective-C functionality, where the third `case` and fourth `case` match, you can add the keyword `fallthrough` to the `case`, and the `case` will not break:

```
var geo = (2,4)
switch geo {
//(anything, 5)
case (_,5):println("It's (Something,5)")
case (5,_):println("It's (5,Something)")
case (1...3,_):
    println("It's (1 2 or 3, Something)")
    fallthrough
case (1...3,3...6):
    println("We will match here too!")
default:println("It's something else")
}
```

Now the third `case` and fourth `case` match, and you get both `println` statements:

```
It's (1, 2 or 3, Something)
We will match here too!
```

Remember the value binding example from earlier? You can use this same idea in `switch` state-ments. Sometimes it's necessary to grab values from the tuple. You can even add in a `where` statement to make sure you get exactly what you want:

```
var geo = (2,4)
switch geo {
case (_,5):println("It's (Something,5)")
case (5,_):println("It's (5,Something)")
case (1...3,let x):
    println("It's (1 2 or 3, \(x))")
case let (x,y):
    println("No match here for \(x) \(y)")
case let (x,y) where y == 4:
    println("Not gonna make it down here either for \(x) \(y)")
default:println("It's something else")
}
```

This is the mother of all `switch` statements. Notice that the last two cases will never run. You can comment out the third then fourth `switch` statement to see each run. We talked about the first `case` and second `case`. The third `case` sets the variable x (to 4) to be passed into the `println` if there is a match. The only problem is that this works like the underscore by accept-ing everything. You can solve this with the `where` keyword. In the fourth `case`, you can declare both x and y at the same time by placing the `let` outside the tuple. Finally, in the last `case`, you want to make sure that you pass the variables into the statement, and you want y to be equal to 4. You control this with the `where` keyword.

Stop...Hammer Time

It's important to have some control over your `switch` statements and loops. You can use `break`, `continue`, and labels to control them.

Using `break`

Using `break` stops any kind of loop (`for`, `for in`, or `while`) from carrying on. Say that you've found what you were looking for, and you no longer need to waste time or resources looping through whatever items remain. Here's what you can do:

```
var mystery = 5
for i in 1...8 {
    if i == mystery {
        break
    }
```

```
    println(i) // Will be 1, 2, 3, 4
}
```

The loop will never print 5 and will never loop through 6, 7, or 8.

Using `continue`

Much like `break`, `continue` will skip to the next loop and not execute any code below the `continue`. If you start with the previous example and switch out `break` with `continue`, you will get a result of 1, 2, 3, 4, 6, 7, and 8:

```
var mystery = 5
for i in 1...8 {
    if i == mystery {
        continue
    }
    println(i) // Will be 1, 2, 3, 4, 6, 7, 8
}
```

Using Labeled Statements

`break` and `continue` are fantastic for controlling flow, but what if you had a `switch` statement inside a `for in` loop? You want to `break` the `for` loop from inside the `switch` statement, but you can't because the `break` you write applies to the `switch` statement and not the loop. In this case, you can label the `for` loop so you can say that you want to break the `for` loop and not the `switch` statement:

```
var mystery = 5
rangeLoop: for i in 1...8 {
    switch i {
    case mystery:
        println("The mystery number was \(i)")
        break rangeLoop
    case 3:
        println("Was three. You have not hit the mystery number yet.")
    default:
        println("was some other number \(i)")
    }
}
```

Here, you can refer to the right loop or `switch` to `break`. You could also `break` for loops within for loops without returning a whole function. The possibilities are endless.

Summary

This chapter has covered a lot of ground. You can see that Swift isn't another version of Objective-C. Swift is a mixture of principles from a lot of languages, and it really is the best of many languages. It has ranges, which pull syntax straight out of Ruby. It has `for in` loops with `enumerate` and tuples, which both are straight out of Python. It has regular `for` loops with `i++` or `++i`, which come from C and many other languages. It also has optionals, which are Swift's own invention.

You'll see shortly that Swift has a lot of cool features that make it easy to use along with your Objective-C and C code. You have already gotten a small taste of arrays. Chapter 2, "Collecting Data," covers arrays and dictionaries in detail. You'll see how Swift's strong typing and optionals come into play.

2

Collecting Data

This chapter explains what Swift has available for collecting and managing data. Objective-C has NSArray *and* NSDictionary *through Cocoa. Swift is compatible and used alongside Objective-C, so you have all those* NS *tools available to you. In addition, you'll also have Swift's native arrays and dictionaries available.*

This chapter describes arrays and dictionaries and the different tools available in each. You will learn how to add and remove elements from collections. You will also learn how Swift's strong type inference allows for quickly written and strongly typed arrays and dictionaries. You will learn when to use NSArrays *and when to use Swift's own arrays.*

Using Arrays

Swift is different from Objective-C in terms of arrays. In Objective-C, you can put whatever you want in an NSArray. In Swift, you must tell Swift exactly what type of things will be going into the array. This makes for extremely predictable code. An array stores multiple values of the same type in a sequential list. You can use Swift's powerful type inference to write arrays quickly, using shorthand notation. You can also declare them verbosely, but you won't see that done very often.

Your First Array

You can create an array by declaring a variable to hold the array and then telling Swift exactly what is going to be in that array. Here's how you do that:

```
var myFirstArray:Array<Int> = Array<Int>()
```

Here you declare the variable myFirstArray, and you declare the variable to be of type Array<Int>. This says that the array is an array of integers. You then set myFirstArray equal to a new array of integers by adding an empty set of parentheses at the end.

> **Note**
>
> Of course you can write this verbose array syntax, but so you will very rarely see arrays written this way because Swift has type inference.

A Quicker Array

Of course you know from Chapter 1, "Getting Your Feet Wet," that Swift has powerful type inference. You don't need to declare an array as verbosely as you did earlier. Here is a quicker way:

```
var quickerArray = [Int]()
```

Here you use `Int` surrounded by square brackets to mean "an array of `Int`s." This syntax was originally written as `Int []` before Xcode beta 3. It was subsequently changed to include the square brackets around the type. If you write it in the old-fashioned way, Xcode will provide an auto-correction for you.

You can also instantiate an array with items directly in it. When you do this, Swift can infer the type of the array so you don't even have to declare a type. Here's how it works:

```
var arrayOfInts = [1,2,3,4]
```

This gives you an array of `Int`s, and if you try to add a `String` to it, Swift complains because Swift is strictly typed:

```
dontInferMe.append("hi")
// Type 'Int' does not conform to protocol 'StringLiteralConvertible'
```

We haven't talked about `append` yet, but you can guess that it adds an item to the array.

Working with arrays in Swift gets even more awesome because you can add any old thing into an array without Swift complaining. Believe it or not, the array will still be strictly typed:

```
var mixedArray = [1,"hi",3.0,Float(4)]
```

Here you have made an array with an `Int`, a `String`, a `Double`, and a `Float`. Notice that Swift does not complain. You can click or tap with three fingers simultaneously in XCode on the variable `mixedArray`, and it will tell you it is of type `NSArray` (see Figure 2.1). Swift is smart enough to change the type to use `NSArrays`, which makes sense because `NSArrays` can contain a mixed bag of stuff.

Figure 2.1   Clicking or tapping with three fingers within XCode brings up more information.

Using `AnyObject`

With Swift you can make an array of `AnyObject`s. You will see this done frequently where something has a return value of `[AnyObject]`. This is a nonspecific type to represent any type of class. Objective-C does not have strictly typed arrays, so in order to interface with Cocoa APIs properly, you need some flexibility to return arrays so that they can contain a mixed bag. You will often see Cocoa APIs return `[AnyObject]`.

What's an Array Made Of?

It is possible to inspect the entire Swift programming language in XCode so you can see exactly how it was created. You should take advantage of this as often as possible. It will teach you how Apple likes code structured, and you will learn how to effectively use different types. To see how to do this, in this section, you'll take a look at an array. You won't understand most of the syntax right now, but we will come back to it later, and I promise that it will all become clear to you. In the playground, write this line of code:

```
var a:Array<Int>
```

This declares a variable that is an array of `Int`s. In fact, you can write any type in place of `Int`. This is because `Array` is declared using generics, which you will learn all about in Chapter 9, "Becoming Flexible with Generics."

Next, hold down the Command key on your keyboard and click on `Array<Int>`. You should see something similar to what is shown in Figure 2.2, depending on your version of Xcode.

```
916  struct Array<T> : MutableCollection, Sliceable {
917      typealias Element = T
918      var startIndex: Int { get }
919      var endIndex: Int { get }
920      subscript (index: Int) -> T
921      func generate() -> IndexingGenerator<[T]>
922      typealias SliceType = Slice<T>
923      subscript (subRange: Range<Int>) -> Slice<T>
924  }
925
```

Figure 2.2   The skeleton of the source for arrays.

We will come back to this code shortly and step through it. For now, just know that this is not fully functioning code. It is just a bunch of declarations that are missing their implementations. One thing you can gain from this code with your current knowledge is that arrays will have a `startIndex` and `endIndex`, which you can grab. If you were to try this out with the `mixedArray` from earlier, it would not work because that is an `NSArray`, not a Swift array. Let's create an example using the start and end index:

```
var ints = [1,2,3,4,5]
ints.startIndex // prints 0
ints.endIndex // prints 5
```

You were able to enter the Swift source code and test something you found in there. Cool!

Differences Between `NSArrays` and **Swift Arrays**

Did you notice in the preceding section that you don't have mutable and immutable versions of the Swift array? Mutable means that something can be changed and immutable means it cannot be changed. An immutable array cannot change once it is created. Well, you really do have mutable and immutable versions of the array and every other variable, but you don't need two different classes for each. To make an immutable array in Swift, you just assign it to a constant with `let`. If you want to make a mutable array in Swift, you just assign it to a variable using the keyword `var`:

```
var mutableArray = [1,2,3,4,5]
let immutableArray = [1,2,3,4,5]
```

The following is a comparison of Swift arrays and Objective-C `NSArray` and `NSMutableArray`:

Language	Type	Mutability
Swift	`let a:Array<Int>`	Immutable
Swift	`var a:Array<Int>`	Mutable
Objective-C	`NSArray`	Immutable
Objective-C	`NSMutableArray`	Mutable

Modifying Arrays

Creating arrays is easy, but what can you do with them? You can append, insert, remove, and iterate over them. You can change them as long as they are mutable.

Accessing Array Elements

You can access elements from an array by using what Swift calls *subscripts*. You will learn much more about subscripting later, but for now, you just need to know that you can use the square brackets notation that you see in many other languages to access elements of an array. Here's an example:

```
var myArray = [1,2,3,4]
myArray[0] // 1
```

Arrays start from an index of 0. Grabbing the 0th element will give you back the first element. You can also use the `startIndex` property of the array to find this out. You can also grab the total number of items in an array by using the `count` method:

```
myArray.count  // 4
```

Adding Elements to an Array

If you have an array of prime numbers and want to add a new prime number to the list, you can use Swift's append method, like this:

```
var primes = [2,3,5,7,11,13,17,19,23,29]
primes.append(31) // [2,3,5,7,11,13,17,19,23,29,31]
```

> **Note**
>
> If you have appended to an array in Python before, you know that Python also uses append to add to arrays. You will see some things in Swift from other languages from time to time.

You can also use += to easily concatenate two arrays:

```
raining += ["dogs","pigs","wolves"] // ["cats","dogs","pigs","wolves"]
```

When you append to an array, you are adding an element to the end of an array. The element you append will always become the last element.

If you want to add an element at the beginning of the array, you can use insert. Maybe it's raining dogs and cats instead of cats and dogs:

```
var raining = ["cats"]
raining.insert("dogs",atIndex: 0)
raining // ["dogs","cats"]
```

Removing Elements from Arrays

If you want to remove items from an array, you can use a number of methods in Swift. For example, you can remove the last item with removeLast():

```
raining.removeLast()
```

And you can remove an element at a specific index by using removeAtIndex(:atIndex):

```
var raining = ["cats","octopuses"] // cats, octopuses
raining.insert("dogs", atIndex: 1)
raining // cats, dogs, octopuses
raining.removeAtIndex(1) // returns the element it removed "dogs"
raining // cats, octopuses
```

Here's what's going on here:

1. You start with an array of two elements.

2. You insert an element at index 1.

3. Then you just remove the same item you added at index 1.

When removing elements from an array it is important to remember that it works like a deck of cards. If you remove the third card from a deck, the fourth card becomes the third card and so on with every card below the fourth card. The second card does stay in the second position.

You can also do the following:

- Create arrays with any type
- Create arrays of mixed types
- Add and remove items at the end of the array

Iterating Over Arrays

When you iterate over an array, you start at the beginning of the array and access each element of the array until you get to the end. Oftentimes you are looking for an element that meets a certain condition. Sometimes you will successfully find that element, and you will not need to iterate any further, so you will break the loop. The `for-in` loop is well suited for interating over arrays. Here's what it looks like:

```
for animal in raining {
    println(animal)
}
// cats
// octopuses
```

Sometimes you need to access the current index for tracking purposes. For this purpose, Swift provides a global `enumerate` function, which gives you access to the current index and current element. Here's how it works:

```
for (i,animal) in enumerate(raining) {
    println("Animal number \(i) is the \(animal)")
}
// Animal number 0 is the cats
// Animal number 1 is the octopuses
```

Extra Bits of Arrays

You can create arrays that are empty or with prepopulated contents. You can create and prepopulate an array by using the extra parameters `extra:` and `repeatedValue:`. Here's an example:

```
var mapRow1 = [Int](count:10,repeatedValue:0) // [0,0,0,0,0,0,0,0,0,0]
```

Here we created a map for a game. If you were using this map for a game, you could place arrays within arrays to create a multidimensional array. You can use one array for each row and place that in one big array, like this:

```
var mapRow1 = [Int](count:10,repeatedValue:0)
var cols = 10
```

```
var rows = 10
var map = [[Int]]()
for row in 0..<rows {
    var newRow = [Int](count:cols, repeatedValue:0)
    map.append(newRow)
}
map
```

In this example, you create an array within an array. So the type of map is [[Int]], which means an array of arrays of Ints. Because [Int] is an array of Ints, wrapping that in square brackets will give you an array of Ints. This type of multidimensional array can be used in games to create a sort of tile map. Maybe for this map 0 is ground, 1 is road, and 2 is tree. The preceding example makes a whole map of ground. Notice that it does so without making a nested for loop.

Emptying an Array

You can completely empty an array by setting it equal to []: This technique is used in other languages.

```
map = []
map // 0 Elements
```

Using Dictionaries

Dictionaries are similar to arrays in that they are both containers that store multiple values of the same type. Dictionaries are different from arrays in that each value is stored with a key. You use that key to access the value. In arrays, you access elements by index. Arrays are stored in a specific order, and dictionaries are not. Just like arrays, though, dictionaries want to know what *type* you will be storing for their values. They also want to know what *type* you will use for its keys. You can write a dictionary in verbose form or shorthand. First the verbose:

```
var people:Dictionary<Int,String> = [186574663:"John Smith",
                                     198364775:"Francis Green",
                                     176354888:"Trevor Kalan"]
people[176354888] // {Some "Trevor Kalan"}
```

This dictionary is of type [Int : String]. Again, you can three-finger-click or tap the variable name to find the *type* of the dictionary. The keys are of *type* Int, and the values are of *type* String. There are a couple things to note here. For one thing, you can access the dictionary by using the same syntax that you use to access arrays. Note that by accessing the dictionary, Swift returns an optional (see Chapter 1). Why does Swift return an optional? It is possible that you are trying to access something that is not there. If you were sure that there is a value at the key you were accessing, you could force the value out with an exclamation point, like this:

```
people[176354888]! // "Trevor Kaleface"
```

Of course, there is a shorthand way to write dictionaries since Swift can automatically infer the *types* of dictionaries. You can rewrite a dictionary without an explicit type, like this:

```
var people = [186574663:"John Smith",
              198364775:"Francis Green",
              176354888:"Trevor Kaleface"]
```

It's still the same dictionary as before.

Adding, Removing, and Inserting with Dictionaries

Previously you used the subscript syntax (the square brackets syntax) to access elements of a dictionary. You can use that syntax to also set values by key. In the previous example, you can set a person with a Social Security number of 384958338:

```
people[384958338] = "Skip Wilson"
```

If the key exists, then you will replace that Social Security value with `Skip Wilson`. If not, you will have a new key/value pair. Try to assign a key using a string, and you get an error.

You can also use the method `updateValue(forKey:)` to update your dictionary. This method also updates a value for a key if it exists, or it creates a new key value if it does not exist. `updateValue` returns an optional, which is the old value it replaced, or `nil` if it did not replace anything.

To remove items from a dictionary, you can just assign it to `nil`:

```
people[384958338] = nil
```

Now the person with Social Security number 384958338 is removed from the dictionary. You can also use `removeValueForKey` to do the same thing. It returns the old value it removed if the key exists. If not, it returns `nil`. It is otherwise known as an optional, and it looks like this:

```
people.removeValueForKey(176354888) // {Some "3343"}
people.removeValueForKey(24601) // nil
```

Iterating Over Dictionaries

You can iterate over a dictionary much the same way that you iterate over an array—by using a `for-in` loop. The only difference between an array `for-in` loop and a dictionary `for-in` loop is that with the dictionary loop, you are able to get both keys and values while looping, like this:

```
for (ssn,name) in people {
    println("SSN: \(ssn) Name: \(name)")
}
// SSN: 198364775 Name: Francis Green
// SSN: 176354888 Name: Trevor Kalan
// SSN: 186574663 Name: John Smith
```

You can also loop through just the keys of a dictionary, with `.keys`. In addition, you can loop though just the values with `.values`:

```
for ssn in people.keys {
    println("SSN: \(ssn)")
}
for name in people.values {
    println("Name: \(name)")
}
```

Extra Bits of Dictionaries

You can create a new dictionary like this:

```
var vehicles = Dictionary<String,String>()
```

It is worth noting that once again, if you Command+click on the dictionary, you will see that it is made up of a `Struct` and subscripts. The `<>` characters tell you that the dictionary is made with generics, and it will accept any *type* at all for its keys and values. (Generics are a powerful feature of Swift. and you will learn much more about them in Chapter 9, "Becoming Flexible with Generics.")

If you want to count the number of key/value pairs in a dictionary, you can use `.count`:

```
people.count // 3
```

Emptying a Dictionary

You can empty a dictionary just by calling `[:]`, like this:

```
people = [:] // 0 key/value pairs
```

Testing Dictionaries for the Presence of Values

Dictionaries return optionals when you try to access items. Therefore, you might want to place them into value bindings. If you don't need the value of the key you are testing, you can instead use a regular `if` statement, like this:

```
if people[198364775] {
    println("Got him")
} else {
    println("No one with that Social Security number")
}
```

If you do in fact want the unwrapped value from the optional (if it does succeed), you can use full value binding, like this:

```
if let person = people[198364775] {
    println("Got \(person)")
```

```
} else {
    println("No one with that social security number")
}
```

Now you will have the unwrapped value of the optional available to you if there is a value to be had.

Putting It All Together

Next, you will create a little program from all the massive amounts of knowledge you have acquired thus far. Enter the code in Listing 2.1.

Listing 2.1   **A Complete Example**

```
import Foundation

let city = "Boston"
let trainName = "the Red Line"

var subwayStops = [
    // Stop name and busyness on a scale of 1-10
    ("Harvard Square", 6),
    ("Kendall / MIT", 5),
    ("Central Square", 7),
    ("Charles MGH", 4),
    ("Park Street", 10)
]

var passengers = 0

for i in 0..<subwayStops.count {
    var (stopName, busyness) = subwayStops[i]
    // New passengers boarding the train
    var board:Int

    switch (busyness) {
    case 1...4: board = 15
    case 5...7: board = 30
    case 7..<9: board = 45
    case 10: board = 50
    default: board = 0
    }

    // Some passengers may leave the train at each stop
    let randomNumber = Int(arc4random_uniform(UInt32(passengers)))
```

```
    //Ensure that passengers never becomes negative
    if randomNumber < passengers {
        passengers -= randomNumber
        println("\(randomNumber) leave the train")
    }

    passengers += board
    println("\(board) new passengers board at \(stopName)")
    println("\(passengers) current on board")
}
println("A total of \(passengers) passengers were left on \(trainName) in \(city)")
```

You can paste this code directly into the playground so you can step through it:

- Line 3: You create a city constant (Boston, in this case).

- Line 4: You create a train name constant.

- Lines 6–13: You create the subway stops array. This is of type [(String, Int)], which means an array of tuples in which the tuples are of types String and Int.

> **Note**
>
> For bonus points, make the array into an array of named tuples or reimplement it as a dictionary.

- Line 15: You specify the current number of passengers.

- Line 17: This is the main game loop, which loops from 0 to the number of subway stops.

- Line 18: You grab values out of the tuples smoothly and simultaneously.

- Line 22: You specify a switch with ranges, based on the busyness of the current stop.

- Lines 23–26: If the busyness level is between x to y, you board z number of people.

- Line 27: You need a default because the switch is not exhaustive. Your passengers might be exhausted, though.

- Line 31: You choose a random number of passengers between 0 and the number of passengers current on the train to leave the train at each stop.

- Line 34: You have to make sure randomNumber is less than the current number of passengers. You make those people leave the train.

- Line 39: You choose the number of passengers to board from the switch statement.

- Line 40: You print the number of new passengers.

- Line 41: You print the number on board.

- Line 44: You finish the game with the total number of passengers left on board.

Summary

With arrays and dictionaries you are able to store data in many different ways. They are like the tools in a carpenter's kit. Arrays and dictionaries are an essential asset to successful Swift programming. Swift has given us multiple ways of accessing, adding, and removing items from these collections. The ways that you can use collections is up to you, and you will find there are many different uses for them.

3

Making Things Happen: Functions

This chapter discusses functions. You will find that Swift functions are based on the best implementations functions in other languages. Swift functions provide you with lots of flexibility to create parameters that are both "internal" and "external," which jives well with Objective-C. Internal and external parameters allow you to have functions that are easy to read. You'll be able to quickly read the name of a function and know exactly what it does. This is one excellent feature of Objective-C that has made its way into Swift.

A function itself can also be passed as a parameter of another function, also known as anonymous functions. This makes it easy to pass parameters around to different contexts. Functions can contain other functions; these are called closures and are discussed in Chapter 6, "Reusable Code: Closures." Closures and functions go hand in hand.

A function groups commonly used code together so that it can be reused as many times as is needed. Say that you have a game in which a character jumps in the air, which is a super common functionality in a game. You would need to write the code to make the character jump. Jumping in games gets rather complicated, and you wouldn't want to rewrite that code every time you wanted the character to jump; handling the jumping character that way would be messy and error prone. Instead, you could create a function to wrap all that jumping code into a nice little package of goodness. Then, instead of writing all that code again, you could just use your `jump()` *function. This is like using a real-life button press to make something work. That button connects to all the functionality contained within the component you're activating. You don't necessarily have to know how it works; you just know that pressing the button will make it work.*

When you think about writing Swift code, you have to realize that there is a lot of functionality that just works. You may never know how it was written or how many lines of code it took to write it. You just know that when you call it, it will work.

For example, calling `countElements` *on the string* `"Hi"` *returns 2, which is the number of characters in the string. You didn't have to write that function. It came with Swift. With Swift, you can write your own functions and then forget how you made them work. Once you've written* `jump()`, *you can call it to have your character jump.*

Defining Functions

In Swift, a function is made up of three components: a name, parameters, and a return type. The syntax for this type of declaration is as follows:

```
func functionName(parameterName: parameterType) -> returnType {
  //code
}
```

This syntax is very different from Objective-C method declarations. However, if you have ever used JavaScript, Python, C, or many other languages, then this syntax will be pretty familiar. You will find that while the structure of functions is different, there are parts that make it compatible with Objective-C.

Let's look at some examples, starting with a function that takes no arguments and has no return values:

```
func sayHello() {
    println("Hello!")
}
```

Here you write the keyword `func` and then name the function `sayHello`. You use `()` to house parameters, when you need them; for now you can leave these parentheses empty. You use curly brackets to contain the code that needs to run when the function is called. To call this function, you simply use its name followed by parentheses. You would call `sayHello` like this:

```
sayHello()
```

This is about as basic a function as you can create. You can go a step further and add an argument that allows the function to "say hello" to a specific person. To do that, you need to allow the function to take a single argument of type `String` that represents a name. That type of declaration might look like this:

```
func sayHello(name: String) {
  println("Hello, \(name)!")
}
```

Now you've added a parameter to the function. That parameter is of type `String` and called name.

> **Note**
>
> If you're following along in your own playground, it isn't necessary to overwrite your old implementation of `sayHello`. The type inference in Swift allows you to differentiate between your different declarations of `sayHello` based on the arguments. This means that if you call this, Swift will infer that you are looking for `sayHello` with no arguments:
>
> ```
> sayHello()
> // Hello!
> ```

If, however, you add an argument of type String to the function call, like this, Swift will now infer that you're looking for the implementation of sayHello that takes one argument of type String:

```
sayHello("Skip")
// Hello, Skip!
```

As long as the argument types, the return types, or both are different, declaring functions with the same name will not cause issues with the compiler. You can actually have multiple functions with the same name sitting in the same file, so you shouldn't erase your other functions.

Next, you'll create another implementation of your sayHello function that says "hello" to someone a certain number of times. This will give you a chance to look at how to declare a function with multiple parameters:

```
func sayHello(name: String, numberOfTimes: Int) {
  for _ in 1...numberOfTimes {
    sayHello(name)
  }
}
```

This function declaration can be read as "a function named sayHello that takes two arguments of type String and type Int with no return value." The syntax is almost identical to that of the single argument function, just with an extra comma added to separate the arguments. You are even using the same name for the function. In fact, you are calling the first implementation of sayHello within the new declaration. Now, if you wanted to use this function, here's how it would look:

```
sayHello("Skip", 5)
//Hello Skip!
//Hello Skip!
//Hello Skip!
//Hello Skip!
//Hello Skip!
```

We'll elaborate a bit more on how Swift differentiates between these declarations when we discuss function types later in the chapter in "Functions as Types," but for now, we're going to move on to adding a return type to the function implementations.

To add a return argument in the function declaration, you simply include the pointer arrow, ->, followed by the return type.

Return Types

Next you'll create a function that returns its sum, which will also be of return type Int:

```
func sum(a: Int, b: Int) -> Int {
  return a + b
}
```

This declaration can be read as "a function, sum, that takes two arguments of type Int and has a return value of type Int." If you wanted to call the new function, it could look something like this:

```
let total = sum(14, 52)
// total = 66
```

Returning a single value is just fine, but sometimes you want to return multiple values. In Objective-C, this problem is usually solved by creating an object class or by returning some sort of collection. These solutions would work in Swift as well, but there is a better way: You can return multiple arguments in Swift by using tuples, as described in the next section.

Multiple Return Values

Like Objective-C functions, Swift functions can return only one value. Unlike Objective-C, though, Swift lets you use tuples as values, which can be useful for packaging together multiple return values so that you can pass around multiple values as one value. Consider a situation where a function is required to return the sum of two numbers as well as the higher of the two. This means that you need the function to returns two values, both of type Int encapsulated in a tuple. Here's what it looks like:

```
func sumAndCeiling(a: Int, b: Int) -> (Int, Int) {
    let ceiling = a > b ? a : b
    let sum = a + b
    return (sum, ceiling)
}
```

You can declare multiple return values by encapsulating them in parentheses, separated by a comma. This is the syntax for a tuple. The preceding function can be read "a function named sumAndCeiling that takes two arguments of type Int and returns a tuple of type (Int, Int)." You can grab values from the returned tuple, from its indexes, like so:

```
let result = sumAndCeiling(4, 52)
let sum = result.0
let ceiling = result.1
```

This is a good way to return multiple values within one function, but using indexes to access values can be confusing. It's also not very pretty, and it's hard to remember which is which. Imagine if someone decided to change the order of the tuples without reading how they were used. It wouldn't be very smart or very nice, and it would severely mess things up. It's more helpful to name the values within a tuple.

Here's how you can modify the sumAndCeiling function with named values within the tuple:

```
func sumAndCeiling(a: Int, b: Int) -> (sum: Int, ceiling: Int) {
    let ceiling = a > b ? a : b
    let sum = a + b
    return (sum, ceiling)
}
```

The syntax for a named tuple is almost identical to the syntax of a parameter. Adding named tuples is an easy way to create more readable code while dealing with fewer errors. Here's a new implementation:

```
let result = sumAndCeiling(16, 103)
let sum = result.sum
// sum = 119
// result.sum == result.0
let ceiling = result.ceiling
// ceiling = 103
// result.ceiling == result.1
```

> **Note**
>
> In general, I prefer accessing tuples by name rather than by index because it is easier to read. This way you always know exactly what the function is returning.

More on Parameters

You already know how to use parameters in functions. As discussed in the following sections, Swift also provides the following:

- External parameter names
- Default parameter values
- Variadic parameters
- In-out parameters
- Functions as parameters

External Parameter Names

Usually you create a function with parameters and just pass them. However, external parameters must be written. Part of what makes Objective-C such a powerful language is its descriptiveness. Swift engineers wanted to also include that descriptiveness, and this is why the language includes external parameter names. External parameters allow for extra clarity. The syntax for including external parameter names in a function looks like this:

```
func someFunction(externalName internalName: parameterType) -> returnType {
  // Code goes here
}
```

The keyword `func` is followed by the name of the function. In the parameters of the function, there's an extra name for the parameters. The whole parameter is an external name followed by an internal parameter followed by the parameter type. The return type of the function follows the function parameters, as usual.

Here's a function that takes the names of two people and introduces them to each other:

```
func introduce(nameOfPersonOne nameOne: String, nameOfPersonTwo nameTwo: String) {
    println("Hi \(nameOne), I'd like you to meet \(nameTwo).")
}
```

Writing this function with external parameters makes it more readable. If someone saw a function called `introduce`, it might not provide enough detail for the person to implement it. With a function called `introduce(nameOfPersonOne:,nameOfPersonTwo:)`, you know for sure that you have a function that introduces two people to each other. You know that you are introducing person one to person two. By adding two external parameters to the function declaration, when you call the `introduce` function, the `nameOfPersonOne` and `nameOfPersonTwo` parameters will appear in the call itself. This is what it looks like:

```
introduce(nameOfPersonOne: "John", nameOfPersonTwo: "Joe")
// Hi John, I'd like you to meet Joe.
```

By including external parameters in functions, you remove the ambiguity from arguments, which helps a lot when sharing code.

You might want your external parameters and internal parameters to have the same name. It seems silly to repeat yourself, and Swift thought it was silly, too. By adding the pound sign (#) as a prefix to an internal parameter name, you are saying that you want to include an external parameter using the same name as the internal one. You could redeclare the `introduce` function with shared parameter names, like so:

```
func introduce(#nameOne: String, #nameTwo: String) {
    println("Hi \(nameOne), I'd like you to meet \(nameTwo).")
}
```

This syntax makes it easy to include external parameters in functions without rewriting the internal parameters. If you wanted to call the `introduce` function, it would look like this:

```
introduce(nameOne: "Sara", nameTwo: "Jane")
// Hi Sara, I'd like you to meet Jane.
```

These external parameters aren't required, but they do make for much greater readability.

Default Parameter Values

Swift supports default parameters unlike in Objective-C where there is no concept of default parameter values. The following is an example of a function that adds punctuation to a sentence, where you declare a period to be the default punctuation:

```
func addPunctuation(#sentence: String, punctuation: String = ".") -> String {
    return sentence + punctuation
}
```

If a parameter is declared with a default value, it will be made into an external parameter. If you'd like to override this functionality and not include an external parameter, you can insert an underscore (_) as your external variable. If you wanted a version of addPunctuation that had no external parameters, its declaration would look like this:

```
func addPunctuation(sentence: String, _ punctuation: String = ".") -> String {
    return sentence + punctuation
}
```

Now you can remove the underscore from the parameters. Then you can call the function with or without the punctuation parameter, like this:

```
let completeSentence = addPunctuation(sentence: "Hello World")
// completeSentence = Hello World.
```

You don't declare any value for punctuation. The default parameter will be used, and you can omit any mention of it in the function call.

What if you want to use an exclamation point? Just add it in the parameters, like so:

```
let excitedSentence = addPunctuation(sentence: "Hello World", punctuation: "!")
// excitedSentence = Hello World!
```

Next you're going to learn about another language feature that allows an unlimited number of arguments to be implemented. Let's talk about variadic parameters.

Variadic Parameters

Variadic parameters allow you to pass as many parameters into a function as your heart desires. If you have worked in Objective-C then you know that doing this in Objective-C requires a nil terminator so that things don't break. Swift does not require such strict rules. Swift makes it easy to implement unlimited parameters by using an ellipsis, which is three individual periods (. . .). You tell Swift what type you want to use, add an ellipsis, and you're done.

The following function finds the average of a bunch of ints:

```
func average(numbers: Int...) -> Int {
    var total = 0
    for n in numbers {
        total += n
    }
    return total / numbers.count
}
```

It would be nice if you could pass in any number of ints. The parameter is passed into the function as an array of ints in this case. That would be [Int]. Now you can use this array as needed. You can call the average function with any number of variables:

```
let averageOne = average(numbers: 15, 23)
// averageOne = 19
let averageTwo = average(numbers: 13, 14, 235, 52, 6)
// averageTwo = 64
```

```
let averageThree = average(numbers: 123, 643, 8)
// averageThree = 258
```

One small thing to note with variadic parameters: You may already have your array of `ints` ready to pass to the function, but you cannot do this. You must pass multiple comma-separated parameters. If you wanted to pass an array of `ints` to a function, you can write the function a little differently. For example, the following function will accept one parameter of type `[Int]`. You can have multiple functions with the same name in Swift, so you can rewrite the function to have a second implementation that takes the array of `ints`:

```
func average(numbers: [Int]) -> Int {
    var total = 0
    for n in numbers {
        total += n
    }
    return total / numbers.count
}
```

Now you have a function that takes an array of `ints`. You might have this function written exactly the same way twice in a row. That works but we are repeating ourselves. You could rewrite the first function to call the second function:

```
func average(numbers: Int...) -> Int {
    return average(numbers)
}
```

Now you have a beautiful function that can take either an array of `ints` or an unlimited comma-separated list of `ints`. By using this method, you can provide multiple options to the user of whatever API you decide to make:

```
let arrayOfNumbers: [Int] = [3, 15, 4, 18]
let averageOfArray = average(arrayOfNumbers)
// averageOfArray = 10
let averageOfVariadic = average(3, 15, 4, 18)
// averageOfVariadic = 10
```

In-Out Parameters

In-out parameters allow you to pass a variable from outside the scope of a function and modify it directly inside the scope of the function. You can take a reference *into* the function's scope and send it back *out* again—hence the keyword `inout`. The only syntactic difference between a normal function and a function with `inout` parameters is the addition of the `inout` keyword attached to any arguments you want to be `inout`. Here's an example:

```
func someFunction(inout inoutParameterName: InOutParameterType) -> ReturnType {
  // Your code goes here
}
```

Here's a function that increments a given variable by a certain amount:

```
func incrementNumber(inout #number: Int, increment: Int = 1) {
    number += increment
}
```

Now, when you call this function, you pass a reference instead of a value. You prefix the thing you want to pass in with an ampersand (&):

```
var totalPoints = 0
incrementNumber(number: &totalPoints)
// totalPoints = 1
```

In the preceding code, a totalPoints variable represents something like a player's score. By declaring the parameter increment with a default value of 1, you make it easy to quickly increment the score by 1, and you still have the option to increase by more points when necessary. By declaring the number parameter as inout, you modify the specific reference without having to assign the result of the expression to the totalPoints variable.

Say that the user just did something worth 5 points. The function call might now look like this:

```
var totalPoints = 0
incrementNumber(number: &totalPoints, increment: 5)
// totalPoints = 5
incrementNumber(number: &totalPoints)
// totalPoints = 6
```

Functions as Types

In Swift, a function is a type. This means that it can be passed as arguments, stored in variables, and used in a variety of ways. Every function has an inherent type that is defined by its arguments and its return type. The basic syntax for expressing a function type looks like this:

```
(parameterTypes) -> ReturnType
```

This is a funky little syntax, but you can use it as you would use any other type in Swift, which makes passing around self-contained blocks of functionality easy.

Let's next look at a basic function and then break down its type. This function is named double and takes an int named num:

```
func double(num: Int) -> Int {
    return number * 2
}
```

It also returns an int. To express this function as its own type, you use the preceding syntax, like this:

```
(Int) -> Int
```

Here you add the parameter types in parentheses, and you add the return type after the arrow.

You can use this type to assign a type to a variable:

```
var myFunc:(Int) -> Int = double
```

This is similar to declaring a regular variable of type `string`, for example:

```
var myString:String = "Hey there buddy!"
```

You could easily make another function of the same type that has different functionality. Just as `double`'s functionality is to double a number, you can make a function called `triple` that will triple a number:

```
func triple(num:Int) -> Int {
    return number * 3
}
```

The `double` and `triple` functions do different things, but their type is exactly the same. You can interchange these functions anywhere that accepts their type. Anyplace that accepts `(Int) -> Int` would accept both the `double` or `triple` functions. Here is a function that modifies an `int` based on the function you send it:

```
func modifyInt(#number: Int, #modifier:(Int) -> Int) -> Int {
    return modifier(number)
}
```

While some languages just accept any old parameter, Swift is very specific about the functions it accepts as parameters.

Putting It All Together

Now it's time to combine all the things you've learned so far about functions. You've learned that the pound sign means that the function has an external parameter named the same as its internal parameter. The parameter modifier takes a function as a type. That function must have a parameter that is an `int` and a return value of an `int`. You have two functions that meet those criteria perfectly: `double` and `triple`. If you are an Objective-C person, you are probably thinking about blocks right about now. In Objective-C, blocks allow you to pass around code similar to what you are doing here. (Hold that thought until you get to Chapter 6.) For now you can pass in the `double` or `triple` function:

```
let doubledValue = modifyInt(number: 15, modifier: double)
// doubledValue == 30
let tripledValue = modifyInt(number: 15, modifier: triple)
// tripledValue == 45
```

> **Note**
>
> This example is obviously completely hard coded, and your examples will be completely dynamic. For example, you would probably replace the number 30 with the current speed of the character when he hits the sonic speed button. For now, you can just settle for 30 and 45.

Listing 3.1 is an example of creating functions in Swift:

Listing 3.1   **A Tiny Little Game**

```swift
var map = [ [0,0,0,0,2,0,0,0,0,0],
            [0,1,0,0,0,0,0,0,1,0],
            [0,1,0,0,0,0,0,0,1,0],
            [0,1,0,1,1,1,1,0,1,0],
            [3,0,0,0,0,0,0,0,0,0]]

var currentPoint = (0,4)
func setCurrentPoint(){
    for (i,row) in enumerate(map){
        for (j,tile) in enumerate(row){
            if tile == 3 {
                currentPoint = (i,j)
                return
            }
        }
    }
}

setCurrentPoint()

func moveForward() -> Bool {
    if currentPoint.1 - 1 < 0 {
        println("Off Stage")
        return false
    }
    if isWall((currentPoint.0,currentPoint.1 - 1)) {
        println("Hit Wall")
        return false
    }
    currentPoint.1 -= 1
    if isWin((currentPoint.0,currentPoint.1)){
        println("You Won!")
    }
    return true
}

func moveBack() -> Bool {
    if currentPoint.1 + 1 > map.count - 1 {
        println("Off Stage")
        return false
    }
    if isWall((currentPoint.0,currentPoint.1 + 1)) {
        println("Hit Wall")
```

```
        return false
    }
    currentPoint.1 += 1
    if isWin((currentPoint.0,currentPoint.1)){
        println("You Won!")
    }
    return true
}

func moveLeft() -> Bool {
    if currentPoint.0 - 1 < 0 {
        return false
    }
    if isWall((currentPoint.0 - 1,currentPoint.1)) {
        println("Hit Wall")
        return false
    }
    currentPoint.0 -= 1
    if isWin((currentPoint.0,currentPoint.1)){
        println("You Won!")
    }
    return true
}

func moveRight() -> Bool {
    if currentPoint.0 + 1 > map.count - 1 {
        println("Off Stage")
        return false
    }
    if isWall((currentPoint.0 + 1,currentPoint.1)) {
        println("Hit Wall")
        return false
    }
    currentPoint.0 += 1
    if isWin((currentPoint.0,currentPoint.1)){
        println("You Won!")
    }
    return true
}

func isWall(spot:(Int,Int)) -> Bool {
    if map[spot.0][spot.1] == 1 {
        return true
    }
    return false
}
```

```
func isWin(spot:(Int,Int)) -> Bool {
    println(spot)
    println(map[spot.0][spot.1])
    if map[spot.0][spot.1] == 2 {
        return true
    }
    return false
}

moveLeft()
moveLeft()
moveLeft()
moveLeft()
moveBack()
moveBack()
moveBack()
moveBack()
```

This is a map game. This game allows the user to navigate through the map by using function calls. The goal is to find the secret present (the number 2). If the player combines the right moves in the move function, he or she can find the secret present. Your current status will read out in the console log.

Let's step through this code:

- Line 1: You have a multidimensional array map, which is an array within an array.

- The function setCurrentPoint finds the 3, which is the starting point, and sets it as the current point.

- You have four directional functions that move the current point's x or y position.

- In each of those functions you check whether you hit a wall using that isWall function.

- In each of those functions you also move the player's actual position.

- After the position is moved you check whether you won the game by seeing whether you landed on a 2.

- You can call each function one by one and the console will trace out whether you won or not. It will not move if you are going to hit a wall. It will also not move if you are going to go off stage.

Summary

This chapter just scratches the surface of using functions in Swift. You learned most of what there is to learn syntactically, but there is more to come with the possibilities of implementation. Now that you know all the different ways to use functions in Swift, it is now time to start experimenting and implementing. Functions are one of the puzzle pieces of object-oriented programming, but you need more pieces to complete the picture. Next you will learn how to turn functions into methods of a class, struct, and enum. You will learn the basic building blocks of structuring code. When combined with classes, structs, and enums, functions become a part of that bigger object-oriented programming picture.

4

Structuring Code: Enums, Structs, and Classes

This chapter covers the basic structural methods of Swift: enums, structs, and classes. With these tools, you are able to more easily organize your code for reuse. You will find yourself typing less code when using these tools properly. Structs, enums, and classes are similar to functions in that they allow you to group some code together for reuse. They are different from functions because they can contain functions.

If you are familiar with Objective-C, C, C++, or Java and other languages, you should know about enums as they are a part of many languages. You write typedef *because in Objective-C and C (but not C++), you have to always precede an enum with the word* enum. *You create a* typedef *to make a shortcut to the enum to reduce the typing. In Swift, you use enum types any time you need to represent a fixed set of constants, including things like the planets in our solar system. You use it in situations where you know all the possible values—for example, menu options or command-line options.*

Structures and classes have a lot of similarities in their intended functionalities. Structs, enums, and classes can have methods, which are functions within the enum, struct, or class. These methods provide that specific object with something it can do. Methods are doers. Methods (which you can think of as functions within classes, structs, or enums) give you some information about the object.

Structs and classes are very similar in that they contain a design for representing objects. The big difference is that structs are always created new or copied when passed around, and classes are passed around by reference. If your friend wanted to borrow something from you, you would definitely lend it to him because you two are best buds. If that to-be-borrowed something were a struct, you would have to pull out the 3D printer and print your friend a brand-new one and hand it over. If that something were a class, you would give your friend a card that told exactly where to find that something anytime he looked for it.

Enums

Enums, structs, classes, and protocols are all written in a very similar way. Here is how you create an enum for the suits in a deck of cards:

```
enum Suit {
    //... enum implementation goes here
}
```

You should choose a singular name (not plural) for the enum—like `Suit` in this case. You write the word `enum` and then give the enum a name and write a pair of curly brackets. The enum implementation goes inside the curly brackets. Here is a simple enum that declares all possible suits in a deck of cards:

```
enum Suit {
    case Hearts
    case Clubs
    case Diamonds
    case Spades
}
```

Now you can declare `Suit.Clubs`:

```
var thisCardSuit = Suit.Clubs
```

Now `thisCardSuit` is of type `Suit`. Each one of the choices is called a "member" of the enum. Each member is a constant and cannot be changed. You want to name your enums so they are easily read. When you read the preceding declaration, you can think of it as saying. "This card suit is a suit which is clubs" (or simplified to "This card suit is clubs"), which reads like a sentence.

If the variable you declare is already declared as a type `Suit`, you do not have to write the full name of the enum. You can use this instead:

```
var thisCardSuit:Suit // declaring the type suit.
thisCardSuit = .Clubs // Because suit is declared, we don't need to write
    Suit.Clubs          // Just .Clubs
```

Notice how you can just write `.Clubs`. A good example of this is `UIImagePickerControllerSourceType`, which you use when allowing the user to choose an image from either the camera (to take a picture right now), saved photo albums, or the photo library. If you were to create a function that took a `UIImagePickerControllerSourceType` as a parameter, then you could pass it just `.Camera`, like this:

```
func showImagePickerForSourceType(imageView:UIImageView,
sourceType:UIImagePickerControllerSourceType) {...

...

}
showImagePickerForSourceType(imageView, .Camera)
```

In this example, you can pass the function .Camera because it knows that sourceType must be of type UIImagePickerControllerSourceType.

Which Member Was Set?

After the sourceType for UIImagePickerControllerSourceType is set, how do you figure out which enum value was set? You use a switch statement. Let's go back to the suits in the deck of cards example. You will reuse the thisCardSuit variable like so:

```
switch thisCardSuit {
case .Hearts:
    println("was hearts")
case .Clubs:
    println("was clubs")
case .Diamonds:
    println("was diamonds")
case .Spades:
    println("was spades")
}
// was clubs
```

Of course, this switch statement must be exhaustive (see Chapter 1, "Getting Your Feet Wet"). This example prints out was clubs.

Associated Values

You will often want to associate a value with a member of an enum. Having the member itself is helpful, but sometimes you need more information. Here's how you could create a Computer enum to get an idea of what I mean:

```
enum Computer {
    //ram and processor
    case Desktop(Int,String)
    //screen size, model
    case Laptop(Int, String)
    //screen size, model, weight
    case Phone(Int, String, Double)
    //screen size, model, weight
    case Tablet(Int, String, Double)
}
var tech:Computer = .Desktop(8, "i5")
```

Here you have made a computer that is of type Computer, with a value of Desktop, with 8 GB of RAM and an i5 processor. Notice how you can give each member value different required associated values. Desktop has Int, String, while Phone has Int, String, and Double. To use this Computer enum in a theoretical app, you would make the user choose a technology. You could have her choose between a desktop, laptop, phone, or tablet. After she chooses, you could specify the RAM and processor. If she chose a desktop, she would provide the screen size and model. If she chose a laptop, phone, or tablet, then she would provide the size, model, and weight.

Now you can check the selected `tech` value by using a `switch` statement and simultaneously grab the associated values:

```
switch tech {
case .Desktop(let ram, let processor):
    println("We chose a desktop with \(ram) and a \(processor) processor")
case .Laptop(let screensize):
    println("We chose a laptop which has a \(screensize) in screen")
default:
    println("We chose some other non important computer.")
}
```

You see here that you can grab the associated values out of the chosen `Computer` member by assigning a constant using `let`. Notice that you have to write `let` twice if the enum member has multiple associated values. Of course, there is a shorthand way to write this without writing `let` twice. Here's a more concise way:

```
switch tech {
case let .Desktop(ram, processor):
    println("We chose a desktop with \(ram) and a \(processor) processor")
case let .Laptop(screensize):
    println("We chose a laptop which has a \(screensize) in screen")
default:
    println("We chose some other non important computer.")
}
```

By placing the keyword `let` after the keyword `case` and before the member, you can declare two constants at once. This makes for cleaner code.

Raw Values

Raw values are different from associated values. You cannot have two of the same raw values in an enum. Raw values also all use the same type. You can use `strings`, `ints`, or any floating-point types. When you use `ints`, the value automatically increments for you. For example, say that you use `ints` as the raw value type. Since the raw value will automatically increment, you can use a shorthand way of declaring enum members on one line:

```
enum Suit:Int {
    case Clubs = 1, Hearts, Diamonds, Spades
}
var chosenSuit = Suit.Diamonds
```

Here you declare the raw value type by adding a colon (:) next to the enum name and writing the type. This is similar to declaring a type for a variable or constant. This example uses `Int` so the value will auto-increment. When you declare a raw value for the enum, you can grab that raw value out of the variable by using .toRaw():

```
chosenSuit.toRaw() // 3
```

The raw value of Diamonds is 3 because of the auto-increment. Clubs is 1, Hearts is 2, Diamonds is 3, and Spades is 4.

Play around with this and change Clubs to any integer you want. Try changing it to 100, or -10, or 0. It still auto-increments perfectly.

You can use fromRaw() to do the opposite of toRaw() by getting the raw value from an integer (or whatever type your enum is). fromRaw() returns an optional of type Suit. Why is it an optional? You might try to grab the member with a raw value of 4000, and that would not exist. However, because fromRaw() gives a suit (in an optional), it's helpful to compare it to *something* rather than just print it out. Here's what it looks like:

```
Suit.fromRaw(3) == chosenSuit // true
```

You can then use value binding to find the member for the raw value:

```
enum Suit:Int {
    case Clubs = 1, Hearts, Diamonds, Spades
}
var result = "Don't know yet."
if let theSuit = Suit.fromRaw(3) {
    switch theSuit {
    case .Clubs:
        result = "You chose Clubs"
    case .Hearts:
        result = "You chose hearts"
    case .Diamonds:
        result = "You chose diamonds"
    case .Spades:
        result = "You chose spades"
    }
} else {
    result = "Nothing"
}
result // You chose diamonds
```

Here you have to do value binding for fromRaw() because it is an optional and could have been nil. Once you get theSuit out of the value binding, assuming it's not nil, you can use your normal switch statement to find the chosen suit. Notice that the result variable was successfully changed even though you scoped it through the if and switch statements.

Structs

Structs (which is short for *structures*) are copied when they're passed around. Classes are passed around by reference. This means that you will never have the same instance of a struct. Conversely, you can have multiple instances of the same class.

Here is what classes and structs have in common:

- Both define properties to store values.
- Both define methods to provide functionality.
- Both provide subscripts to give access to their values.
- Both provide initializers to allow you to set up their initial state.
- Both can be extended to provide additional functionality beyond a default implementation. (This is different from inheritance.)
- Both have the ability to conform to protocols (which you will learn about in Chapter 8).

> **Note**
>
> Do not worry too much if you don't understand everything in these lists. You will understand it all by the end of this chapter or in later chapters.

The following are the differences between classes and structs:

- Classes have inheritance.
- Classes have type checking.
- Structs have deinitializers so you can free up unused instances.
- Structs have reference counting. You can have more than one reference to a class instance.

Here's an example of a simple struct:

```
struct GeoPoint {
    var lat = 0.0
    var long = 0.0
}
```

This defines a new struct of type `GeoPoint`. You give the struct two properties and declare them as `doubles`. (Even though you don't see any explicit type declaration, it is happening because `0.0` is inferred as a `double`.)

Now you can use the new struct. If you want to interact with the `GeoPoint` struct, you must create a `GeoPoint` instance:

```
var somePlaceOnEarth = GeoPoint()
```

Now you can interact with the new `GeoPoint` struct, using the dot syntax:

```
somePlaceOnEarth.lat = 21.11111
somePlaceOnEarth.long = 24.232323
```

Notice that when you created a new `GeoPoint` struct, the code completion gives you the option to initialize it with properties (see Figure 4.1).

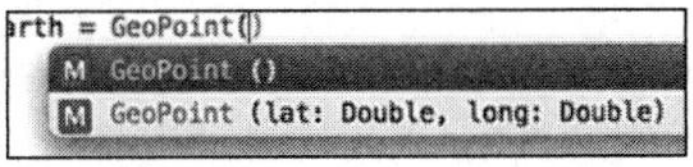

Figure 4.1   Code complete for GeoPoint shows multiple initializers.

You can also write the last three lines as one line:

```
var somePlaceOnEarth = GeoPoint(lat: 21.1111, long: 24.23232)
```

Defining Methods in Structs

When we say *methods*, we are talking about the functions within structs. Methods are just functions that are going to be associated with the structs. By defining a method within the curly brackets of a struct, you are saying that this function belongs to this struct.

Here's an example of a struct with `Point`, `Size`, and `Rect`, which will based on `CGRect`:

```
struct Point {
    var x:Int, y:Int
}

struct Size {
    var width:Int, height:Int
}

struct Rect {
    var origin:Point, size:Size

    func center() -> Point {
        var x = origin.x + size.width/2
        var y = origin.y + size.height/2

        return Point(x: x, y: y)
    }
}
```

The first thing to note is that you declared all the variables on one line. You can use this simplified version of declaring variables where it makes your code more readable. For example, this:

```
var one = 1,two = 2, three = 3
```

is the same as this:

```
var one = 1
var two  = 2
var three = 3
```

You might also notice that you set types for the properties explicitly (for example, `origin:Point, size:Size`). You did not give your properties any default values so Swift would be unable to determine the types of these properties.

However, because you did not give `Rect` any default value, Swift will complain. If you try to make a new `Rect` without any default values in the initializer, you will get an error:

```
var rect:Rect = Rect() // error: missing argument for parameter 'origin' in call
```

Swift does not like that you did not initialize the properties in the struct itself and did not initialize the properties upon making a new `Rect`.

The initializer included with every struct is called a *memberwise initializer*. Memberwise initializers are part of a much larger concept that we won't cover here. When creating a `Rect`, you can use the memberwise initializer to get rid of the error:

```
var point = Point(x: 0, y: 0)
var size = Size(width: 100, height: 100)
var rect:Rect = Rect(origin: point, size: size)
rect.size.height
rect.center()
```

That's better! Since you used the memberwise initializers when constructing `Point`, `Size`, and `Rect`, you no longer get errors. Here you also used the `center()` method of the `Rect`, and it told you that the center of the `Rect` is {x 50 y 50}.

Structs Are Always Copied

Earlier we talked about how structs are always copied when they are passed around. Let's take a look at an example that proves this, using the `Point` struct because it's super simple:

```
var point1 = Point(x:10, y:10)
```

Now you can create `point2` and assign it to `point1`:

```
var point2 = point1
```

You modify `point2`:

```
point2.x = 20
```

Now `point1` and `point2` are different:

```
point1.x // 10
point2.x // 20
```

If `point1` and `point2` were classes, you would not get different values because classes are passed by reference.

Mutating Methods

If a method inside a struct will alter a property of the struct itself, it must be declared as `mutating`. This means that if the struct has some property that belongs to the struct itself (not a local variable inside a method) and you try to set that property, you will get an error unless you mark that method as `mutating`. Here's a struct that will throw an error:

```
struct someStruct {
    var property1 = "Hi there"
    func method1() {
        property1 = "Hello there" // property1 belongs to the class itself
            so we can't change this with making some changes
    }
    // ERROR: cannot assign to 'property1' in 'self'
}
```

The fix for this error is simple. Just add the word `mutating` in front of the `func` keyword:

```
struct someStruct {
    var property1 = "Hi there"
    mutating func method1() {
        property1 = "Hello there"
    }
    // does not throw an error! YAY
}
```

Now that this is fixed, let's take a look at what this error means:

```
cannot assign 'property1' in 'self'
```

Well, it is `property1` that you are trying to modify. This error says that you cannot assign `property1` to self. What is `self`? `self` in this case is the struct's own instance. In this struct, `property1` belongs to an instance of the struct. You could rewrite the line with `property1` to be `self.property1`. However, `self` is always implied, so you don't need to write it. Also notice that the following code works without the `mutating` keyword:

```
struct someStruct {
    func method1() {
        var property2 = "Can be changed"
        property2 = "Go ahead and change me"
    }
}
```

The reason you can set `property2` is because it does not belong to `self` directly. You are not modifying a property of `self`. You are modifying a local variable within `method1`.

Classes

In the following example of creating a class, notice that it looks just like a struct but with the word `class`:

```
class FirstClass {
    // class implementation goes here
}
```

You create a class exactly the same way you create a struct, but instead of using the word `struct`, you use the word `class`. Adding properties to a class is very similar. For example, the following `Car` class has properties for the make, model, and year (and you will define a default value for each property):

```
class Car {
    let make = "Ford"
    let model = "Taurus"
    let year = 2014
}
```

In this example, there are three immutable properties of the `Car` class. Remember that when you make a struct, you are able to leave these properties blank. If you do the same for a class, you get an error:

```
class Car {
    let make:String
    let model:String
    let year:Int
}
// error: class 'Car' has no initializers
```

If you want to fix this error, you must create an initializer for the `Car` class and initialize all the uninitialized properties. Classes in Swift don't have automatic initialization (that is, member-wise initializers). If you leave the properties without default values, you must provide an initializer for the class. Each of the uninitialized properties must be initialized.

Swift provides a global function `init()` for this very purpose. Some languages call this a *constructor*.

Initialization

Initialization is the process of getting the instance of a class or structure ready for use. In initialization, you take all things that do not have values and give them values. You can also do things like call methods, and do other initializations. The big difference between Objective-C initializers and Swift initializers is that Swift initializers do not have to return `self`. The goal of Swift initializers is to give a value to everything that does not have a value. Structs can define initializers even though they have their own memberwise initializers. You can also define multiple initializers for a class or struct. The simplest type of initializer is one without any parameters. They are used to create a new instance of its type. Here's an initializer for the `GeoPoint` class you created earlier:

```
struct GeoPoint {
    var lat:Double
    var long:Double
    init() {
        lat = 32.23232
        long = 23.3434343
    }
}
```

Here you are initializing `lat` and `long` with default values. You could put anything you want in that `init` method.

You can also make multiple initializers so that the user can create a `GeoPoint` however he wants:

```
struct GeoPoint {
    var x = 0.0
    var y = 0.0
    var length = 0.0
    init() {

    }
    init(x:Double,y:Double) {
        self.x = x
        self.y = y
    }
    init(length:Double) {
        self.length = length
    }
}
var regularPoint = GeoPoint()
var pointWithSize = GeoPoint(x: 2.0, y: 2.0)
var otherPoint = GeoPoint(length: 5.4)
```

Now you can initialize `Point` in three different ways. If you want to create a `Point` by using x and y, you can use the initializer `Point(x:Double,y:Double)`. If you want to create a `Point` by length, we could initialize it with `Point(length:Double)`. If you just want to make a standard point, you could initialize it with no parameters to the `init` method. You would probably add more calculations than shown here, but this is the gist of making multiple initializers. As long as the parameters are different, you can make as many different initializers as you need. SpriteKit's `SKScene` has multiple initializers for multiple situations (see Figure 4.2).

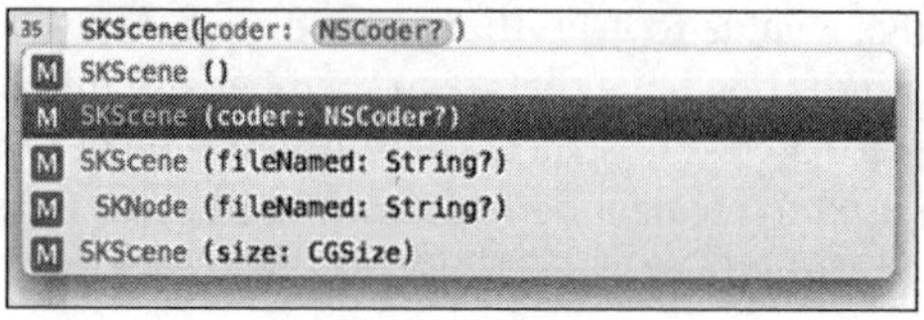

Figure 4.2   SKScene has multiple initializers available.

Here you can see that you can initialize SKScene by filename, by size, and by coder. All this information about multiple initializers applies to both classes and structs. It just so happens that all the examples here use structs.

What Is a Reference Type?

Earlier we said that structs are copied when they are passed around. The other way to say this is that structs are *value types*, and classes are *reference types*. This means that when you assign a variable to a new instance of a class and then reassign that variable to another variable, you have the same reference in each copy of the class. Here's an example:

```
class Car {
    var name = "Honda"
}
var car1 = Car()
var car2 = car1
car1.name = "Dodge" // Dodge
car2.name // Dodge
```

Cool! Notice that when you change car1.name to "Dodge", car2.name is also changed. That is because both car1 and car2 have a reference to the new instance of the Car. If you had done this with a struct, then car1 and car2 would have different values for name.

Do I Use a Struct or a Class?

Whether you need to use a struct or class depends on a few factors, summarized here:

If you say...	you should use a struct	you should use a class
I am storing a few simple data values. Maybe just a few primitives...	×	
I want values to be copied when they are passed around.	×	
I want the properties of my object to also be copied when passed around (a.k.a. value types).	×	
Anything else		×

You can see that you will mostly be using classes for your data structures. Here are a couple examples of good uses of structs:

- A geometric point that contains an x and y and maybe a length
- A geolocation that defines latitude and longitude
- A geometric shape (like `CGRect`) that will contain width and height.

All these structs are simple and contain only a few simple data values (you are not limited to geometric data). They often represent single values like a point or a rectangle.

Forgot Your Pointer Syntax?

When working with C, C++, or Objective-C, you know that you use pointers to reference the address (that is, the location in memory) of some value. You do this in Objective-C by using an asterisk (*). When you create a variable or constant in Swift that references some instance you created, you are not directly accessing that memory address. It is similar to a pointer but not exactly the same. Either way, you never have to reference anything using a pointer syntax when writing Swift.

The reason value types are called *value types* is that they are passed around as actual values. Reference types are called so because they are passed around as references that point to the actual objects. It's the difference between using cash and using checks. When you use cash, you are handing the person actual money (analogous to using value types). When you give someone a check, you are giving him or her not the cash itself but a piece of paper telling where to get the cash (analogous to using reference types). If you think about it, most people pass around money by reference rather than by value. They don't usually deal with the cash itself; they deal with some reference to money.

Property Observers

Property observers are a super-awesome feature built directly into Swift. They allow you to track and reply to changes of a property. You can add property observers to any property except lazy properties, which you won't learn about here. Here's how you create a basic property observer:

```
class Car {
    var name:String = "Honda" {
    willSet(newName) {
        println("About to set the new name to \(newName)")
    }
    didSet(oldName) {
        println("We just set 'name' to the new name \(name) from the old name
            \(oldName)")
    }
    }
}
var car1:Car = Car()
```

```
car1.name = "Ford"
// About to set the new name to Ford
// just set name to the new name Ford from the old name Honda
```

Notice that you add a pair of curly brackets at the end of the variable. Inside those curly brackets you add `willSet` and `didSet`. `willSet` will get called before the property is set. The parameter passed into the function is the new value that the property will be set to. `didSet` will get called after the property is set. The parameter passed into the function is the old value that the property had before it got changed. Obviously, you can access the new value now because it has already been changed.

Methods in Classes

A method and a function are very similar except for a couple differences (aside from scope issues):

- A method has a reference to the object that it belongs to.
- A method is able to use data contained within the class it belongs to.

A method is identical to a function in syntax. Type methods in Swift are similar to Objective-C class methods. A big difference between from C and Objective-C to Swift is that in Swift you can define methods on classes, structs, and enums. This gives you great flexibility and strength. In Swift you have a couple different types of methods available to you. Let's start with instance methods.

Instance Methods

Instance methods are likely the type of methods you will be creating most of the time. An instance method belongs to an instance of a struct, a class, or an enum. It has access to information about that specific instance. It provides functionality to that instance. Earlier you made a `Car` class that had a property name. You could provide it with an instance method to make it go. Then each car you create (or instantiate) will have its own distance that it has traveled. Here's what it would look like:

```
class Car {
    var name = "Ford"
    var distance = 0
    func gas() {
        _spinWheels()
    }
    func _spinWheels() {
        //some complicated car stuff goes here.
        distance += 10
    }
}
var car1 = Car()
println(car1.distance) // 0
car1.gas()
car1.distance // 10
```

Just as in a real car, the details of how a car works are hidden away in this example in a private function. For example, you don't know how the gas pedal on the car works but you know that if you press it the car will go. Obviously, this is not truly necessary in this case, but you can imagine how the details of making a car move forward could get much more complicated. gas and _spinWheels are both instance methods that belong to this specific instance of Car. You know this is true because if you create another car and check the distance, it will not be at the same distance as car1. These methods are acting on *this* instance. For example here is a new car:

```
var car2 = Car()
println(car2.distance) // 0
```

Property Access Modifiers

In the last example you marked a method with an initial underscore to say "Don't use this method outside this class." Swift has three property access modifiers—that is, three ways of forcing the use of a method into a context:

- private entities can be accessed only from within the source file in which they are defined.
- internal entities can be accessed anywhere within the target where they are defined.
- public entities can be accessed from anywhere within the target and from any other context that imports the current target's module.

Without a property access modifier applied, functions are internal. Meaning that if you don't write public or private or internal on the function, it will operate as if you wrote internal.

In the last example it would be more appropriate to change the method _spinWheels to be private and change the name to just spinWheels. You should do this even though you are working in the playground, so private won't restrict access because it's all in the same file.

Type (Static) Methods

In Swift you have instance methods, and you have type methods. Whereas instance methods work on the instance of class, type methods work on the class itself. If you made an instance of the Car class and you had created a type method, you would not be able to use it on the instance of the Car class. These methods are only for the class itself. To add a type method to a class, you use the keyword class. To add a type method to a struct, you use the keyword static, as shown here:

```
class Car {
    var name = "Ford"
    var distance = 0

    class func getCarVersion() -> String {
        return "5.0.1"
    }
}
```

```
var car1 = Car()
println(car1.distance)
Car.getCarVersion()
```

Notice that if you want to access the car version, you call the method on the `Car` class itself. You may see these types of methods used on utilities and in various other situations.

Get to Know Thy `Self`

You use the keyword `self` quite often in Swift. `self` is available on each instance of an object. `self` refers to the current instance. You don't always have to write `self` because Swift implies it. For the `Car` class, you could instead write this:

```
func spinWheels() {
    self.distance += 10
}
```

By using `self.distance` to refer to the distance, you are saying, "distance that belongs to this instance of the class." However, Swift already knows that is what you want, so you can just leave it as `distance`. It is often helpful to use `self` to distinguish between a method parameter and a property of the class, as shown here:

```
class Car {
    var name = "Ford"
    var distance = 0
    func go(distance:Int) {
        self.distance += distance
    }
}
```

In this case, the function has a parameter that is the same as the property of the class. To distinguish between them, you use `self.distance` to mean the property that belongs to the class, and you use just plain `distance` to mean the parameter of the function.

Inheritance: Creating a Bichon from a Dog from an Animal

In my younger and more vulnerable years, my father gave us a dog that we named Penny. She was a Bichon Frise, and we often called her *Le Fluf* (in fake French). Penny provides an excellent example of inheritance. Penny was a Bichon Frise, which is a dog, which is an animal. You could get even more generic, but it's not necessary at this point.

In Swift, a class (the subclass) can inherit methods and properties of another class (the superclass). In our Bichon example, animal is the superclass, and dog is a subclass of animal. Then dog is a superclass of Bichon Frise, which is a subclass of Dog which is a subclass of Animal. In Objective-C, everything eventually inherits from `NSObject`. It's like `NSObject` is 42 (the answer to life, the universe, and everything). It's the base of all superclasses. Swift does not have one grand base class. Defining a class that doesn't inherit from anything makes that class the base class for all other classes that inherit from it. In the following example you create a `Bichon` class, which inherits from the `Dog` class, which inherits from the `Animal` class. In this example, the `Animal` class has its own properties and methods that all its subclasses inherit:

```
class Animal {
    var name:String
    var numberOfLegs:Int
    func move() -> String{
        return "\(name) is moving."
    }
    init(name:String,numberOfLegs:Int) {
        self.name = name
        self.numberOfLegs = numberOfLegs
    }
}


class Dog:Animal {
    var breed:String
    override func move() -> String {
        return "\(name) the \(breed) is moving."
    }
    init(name: String, numberOfLegs: Int,breed:String) {
        self.breed = breed
        super.init(name: name, numberOfLegs: numberOfLegs)
    }
}
class Bichon:Dog {
    var fluffynessLevel:Double
    init(name: String, numberOfLegs: Int, breed: String, fluffynessLevel:Double) {
        self.fluffynessLevel = fluffynessLevel
        super.init(name: name, numberOfLegs: numberOfLegs, breed: breed)
    }
}
var penny = Bichon(name: "Penny", numberOfLegs: 4, breed: "Bichon",
    fluffynessLevel: 100.1)
penny.move() // "Penny the Bichon Frise is moving."
```

This example introduces a couple new concepts. First is `super`. Calling `super` is like calling `self`, except instead of it referring to the instance of the current class, it refers to the instance of the parent class. So if `Bichon` inherits from `Dog`, then `self` would be `Bichon`, and `super` would be an instance of `Dog`.

If you are going to have a class inherit from another class, you should call the initializer of that class along with your class's initializer. `Bichon` is the not the one doing the initialization of name; `Animal` is. So you call `super.init`, which calls the initialization of the parent, which needs to be called again from `Dog` to initialize `Animal`. It is as if you are instantiating the `Dog` class from the `Bichon` class and the `Animal` class from the `Dog` class. You are in fact doing just that, except you won't wind up with three classes in the end. You'll wind up with three parts that make up the `Bichon` class. Kind of like in real life. There are parts of you that are unique to you. Some parts you got from your father. Some parts you may have even gotten from your grandfather, and you made them unique. This is the purpose of overriding. You take something that existed in the parent class and override it with your own implementation. In this case, you just overrode the `move` class to give it a more appropriate implementation from the `Dog` class. It makes sense to add more details to `move` since you are no longer just talking about any kind of `Animal`. You are talking about a `Dog`. As it turns out, for this small program, the dog implementation of `move` is good enough that you don't have to override it in the `Bichon` class.

Summary

In this chapter you've learned how to write enums, structs, and classes. You've learned how to instantiate those classes and how they each react differently to being passed around. We learned about passing by reference as opposed to by value. We also took a look the difference between methods and functions.

5

Making a Game

Now that we've covered user input, events, and data structures in Swift, you're ready to put the concepts into action. In this chapter you'll make a tic-tac-toe game featuring tappable buttons and artificial intelligence (AI). To develop and run it as an iOS app, you'll set up a full-fledged project in Xcode. The IDE makes it easy to add pictures to the game, build a user interface, and respond to player events. If you've built iOS apps in the past, some of the Xcode information in this chapter may be a recap for you. When we move on to the actual game logic, you'll notice a departure from Objective-C. Swift features like type inference really start to shine as you get into bigger and more complex apps.

Building a User Interface (UI)

To start building a game, you need to begin by creating a new Xcode project for the game, which you do by following these steps:

1. Open Xcode 6 and click Create New Xcode Project.

2. Under the iOS > Application tab, select Single View Application (see Figure 5.1).

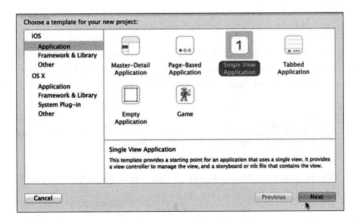

Figure 5.1   The app choosing screen for XCode.

Selecting this option starts you off with a class called a *view controller*. The class links UI events such as button taps to the application logic. For apps that store data, the controller often serves as a link between the user and the model where info is stored.

This paradigm is known as *Model–View–Controller*, or *MVC*. It's a broad topic, but knowing the basics will help you understand how iOS apps are organized. You can think of the controller as a waiter or waitress in a restaurant. He or she interprets orders from a patron (the user) and passes them along to the kitchen (a model). When data or logic pops out of the oven, the controller presents it back to the table (a UI) for the user to consume.

To continue setting up a single view application, you click Next and then follow these steps:

1. Set Product Name to *Swift-Tac-Toe* and Organization Identifier to *com.swiftallmightly.Tic-Tac-Toe*. Be sure to select Swift as your language and iPhone as your device. Deselect Use Core Data.

2. Click Create to open a dialog for naming and saving your project. Then uncheck Create Git Repository.

3. Under the Deployment Info section of the project, check only Portrait for Device Orientation. To keep this exercise simple, disallow Landscape view.

4. In the Interface Builder section of the right panel, uncheck Use Auto Layout. Ensure that Keep Class Size Data For is set to iPhone and then click Disable Class Sizes.

5. In the upper-left corner, next to where Xcode lists the project's name, is a drop-down menu of devices. Choose iPhone 5s.

Congratulations! You've created your first Swift project for iOS.

Importing Assets

Assets O: http://goo.gl/4T1NxG

Assets X: http://goo.gl/f7r45A

Assets bg: http://goo.gl/c6FZPu

Now that you've created a project, the left-hand panel of Xcode should show a list of project files. The center pane shows a white screen representing an iPhone. You can spice things up by preparing images for the blank canvas. Here are the specific UI assets you'll incorporate into the game:

Asset Name	Description
o	O appears in tiles picked by the player
x	X marks tiles chosen by the AI opponent
bg	Features nine black boxes to serve as borders for buttons

To import the assets into your project, select the Image Assets folder from the list of project files in the left-hand panel. Select the New Image button near the bottom of the editor and then click New Image Set. The first picture to place is for the grid. Xcode accepts two versions of this: a normal-sized version (320 × 568 pixels) and one that's twice as large (640 × 1136 pixels) for higher-resolution iPhones. After you drag and drop the images onto the 1x and 2x spots, the background asset is ready. The process for importing the X and the O is the same except that the 2x versions aren't necessary.

Adding Buttons and Labels

Now that you've prepared pictures, it's time to display them as UI elements that players can see and select. You can add a Game Status label and Reset button, too, though these elements aren't linked to images. Start by navigating to `Main.storyboard` in the Xcode project inspector. You should see the blank canvas where you'll place your grid. Locate the search bar in the bottom-right corner of the editor and type in `UI Image View`. Xcode returns a result, which you can drag and drop onto the main workspace.

Stretch the `UIImageView` until it fills the screen. After you've resized the element, click it and look for the Attributes inspector in the upper-right corner. Be sure to uncheck the User Interaction Enabled option under the View panel. You want players to tap buttons on the grid, but they shouldn't be allowed to select the grid itself. Next to the Image field under the Image View panel, type `bg` and press Enter. This links the UI element to the grid image.

It's important to preview your app. Try clicking the play symbol in the upper-left corner of Xcode. If your project is set up correctly, a picture of a black grid will appear in the iOS Simulator (see Figure 5.2). It's a good idea to preview your app often as you work through this chapter. Running the project after each small round of changes will help you pinpoint errors.

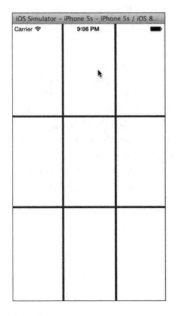

Figure 5.2   Our initial tic-tac-toe board.

You need to create nine other UIImageViews: one to cover each tile in the grid. The background is 320 pixels wide and 568 pixels tall. To find the dimensions of each tile, simply divide by 3. This gives you a width of 106 and a height of 189. You can adjust the tile's size in the measurements section of the Attributes inspector. To find this section, select the tile and click the ruler icon near the upper-right corner of Xcode. You don't have to manually adjust each of the tiles. Just copy and paste the original until you have nine of them, one covering each white space in the grid. Finally, you will need to set the "tag" property for each of the nine additional UIImageViews you just added. The first one will have a tag value of "0," the next "1," and so on. The final UIImageView will have a tag value of "8." To set the tag, click on the UIImageView in your storyboard. Then, in the Attributes Inspector, change the value that appears in the "Tag" field.

Next, you have to tell iOS to listen for tap events. It's possible to make the UIImageViews directly tappable, but for learning purposes, you'll instead use the Button UI element. Using buttons is a flexible solution for capturing touch events, and you're likely to use them in future Swift projects. Find the element and drag it to the workspace in the same way you fetched UIImageView. Adjust the button's width and height so that it covers one of the tiles. By default, it displays the word *Button* in bright blue. The text is unnecessary because the game needs to display an X and an O instead. Click the button to reveal its properties in the Attributes inspector and erase the placeholder text.

To cover the rest of the game board with buttons, you can copy and paste them just as you copied the UIImageViews. At this point, you might find it hard to select buttons because the UI includes quite a few overlapping elements. Instead of clicking the buttons directly, you click their names from a list of UI resources in the View Controller Scene panel. If you preview the app again, you'll notice that the buttons and UIImageViews aren't visible. Rest assured; your hard work hasn't been lost! The buttons will appear later on, when you link them to X and O images.

The last step in creating the user interface is to make a label and a Reset button. To fetch a label element, you repeat the process of finding a UIImageView, but you search instead for Label. After you drag the label onto the main storyboard, stretch it into a bar that spans the whole width of the screen. Add one more button and change its text to *Reset*. Bear in mind that the Reset button and label will overlap the thick black lines of the background grid. You can tweak their background colors in the Attributes inspector to make them stand out. Just below the text options in that panel, there's a check box to make each element hidden by default. Make sure this is checked. The elements will only appear at certain points in the game. When you're finished arranging all the UI elements, your main storyboard should look as shown in Figure 5.3.

Figure 5.3   Our tic-tac-toe board is ready for Xs and Os.

The Action-Packed View Controller

Now that you've developed a working user interface, you can jump into the action: weaving UI elements like buttons and image views into the game logic. In this section, you'll learn how to represent UI elements as resources in the view controller class. As you write class methods to change the resources, making pictures and text appear, the game will spring to life.

Click the tuxedo icon near the upper-right corner of Xcode to enter a side-by-side view. The main storyboard featuring the UI appears on the right. An editor panel appears on the left, showing the default code for the controller class:

```
import UIKit

class ViewController: UIViewController {
    override func viewDidLoad() {
        super.viewDidLoad()
    }

    override func didReceiveMemoryWarning() {
        super.didReceiveMemoryWarning()
        // Dispose of any resources that can be recreated.
    }
}
```

In Chapter 4, "Structuring Code: Enums, Structs, and Classes," you learned that functions and variables can be placed inside—or *encapsulated* within—a class. Classes help you group related functionality and control access to data.

> **Note**
>
> The benefits of using classes may not be obvious at first in small apps, but imagine yourself expanding on this game. If you wrote classes to represent, say, additional players, each player class might try to change buttons and send messages to the UI. *Encapsulating* this stuff in one class makes it easier to control when and how the changes occur.

Notice that the `ViewController` includes two default methods. iOS will call the `viewDidLoad` method when the UI is ready. Logic for initializing the game should go here. The system will call `didReceiveMemoryWarning` if your app overuses or misuses resources. At this point, you can leave this default function alone.

You need to represent your `UIImageViews` as member variables of the `ViewController`. Take a look at your list of UI resources in the panel to the left of the main storyboard. Rename each `UIImageView` that represents a tile (all except the background grid). Call the elements `ticTacImage`, followed by a number related to the element's place on the game board. Moving from top to bottom and left to right, name the tiles `ticTacImage1`, `ticTacImage2`, and so on. For the Reset button and label, use the names `resetBtn` and `userMessage`. After you name the resources, you're free to reference them in your code. Add the following lines to `ViewController`:

```
@IBOutlet var ticTacImage1: UIImageView!
@IBOutlet var ticTacImage2: UIImageView!
@IBOutlet var ticTacImage3: UIImageView!
@IBOutlet var ticTacImage4: UIImageView!
@IBOutlet var ticTacImage5: UIImageView!
@IBOutlet var ticTacImage6: UIImageView!
@IBOutlet var ticTacImage7: UIImageView!
@IBOutlet var ticTacImage8: UIImageView!
@IBOutlet var ticTacImage9: UIImageView!

@IBOutlet var resetBtn : UIButton!
@IBOutlet var userMessage : UILabel!

var plays = [Int:Int]()
var done = false
var aiDeciding = false
var ticTacImages:[UIImageView] = []
```

The `@IBOutlet` keyword tells Xcode that you want to link the variables to UI elements. Just below the `@IBOutlet` references is an array called `plays`. While this isn't directly related to the UI, it helps manage the overall game logic. The array is set up to hold pairs of integers. The first number in each pair represents the position of a tile. The second integer tells which player "owns" the tile: one for a human and zero for the AI. Finally, you define simple Boolean variables called done and aiDeciding. The variable done will equal true only when a player wins or the game is tied. You can probably guess what aiDeciding means. Later in this chapter, when you start building an AI, the variable will stop humans from picking tiles if the AI is still deciding.

Displaying the Player's Moves

Having defined the UIImageViews in code, you can dynamically display some images. The goal is to show an X image on tiles that the user taps and an O on tiles tapped by the AI. "Tapped" is a figure of speech here, of course, because an algorithm will decide which tiles the computer player picks. Don't worry too much about AI for now. You'll learn about that algorithm in the next section, after we finish laying the groundwork for UI events.

For now, you need to detect when a human player taps a tile, so use this code:

```
enum Player: Int {
    case ComputerPlayer = 0, UserPlayer = 1
}

override func viewDidLoad() {
    super.viewDidLoad()
    ticTacImages = [ticTacImage1, ticTacImage2, ticTacImage3,
                    ticTacImage4, ticTacImage5, ticTacImage6, ticTacImage7,
                    ticTacImage8 ,ticTacImage9]
    for imageView in ticTacImages {
        imageView.userInteractionEnabled = true
        imageView.addGestureRecognizer(UITapGestureRecognizer(
        target: self, action: "imageClicked:"))
    }

}

func imageClicked(reco: UITapGestureRecognizer) {
    var imageViewTapped = reco.view as UIImageView

    if plays[imageViewTapped.tag] == nil && !aiDeciding && !done {
        setImageForSpot(imageViewTapped.tag, player:.UserPlayer)
        checkForWin()
        aiTurn()
    }

}

func setImageForSpot(spot:Int,player:Player){

var playerMark = player == .UserPlayer ? "x" : "o"
```

```
        println("setting spot \(player.toRaw()) spot \(spot)")
        plays[spot] = player.toRaw()

        ticTacImages[spot].image = UIImage(named: playerMark)
}
```

You begin by organizing UIImageView references for the tiles into the ticTacImages array. In this case, the array makes it easier for you to change certain tiles. Looping through ticTacImages, the code tells iOS to make each tile element tappable, but what should happen after a tap? To answer this question, take a look at the "action" parameter of UITapGestureRecognizer, a native object. It accepts the function imageClicked as an argument and uses it to handle gesture events. The if statement inside imageClicked puts to use variables defined at the end of the last section. It poses three questions whenever a user taps a tile:

- **Has the tile been tapped before?** To perform this check, you have to find the number of the selected tile. The tag property that we added to the UIImageViews provides this info. The UIImageView is passed in as imageViewTapped. Next our code passes the tile number to the plays array to see what, if anything, matches it. If the query returns an integer, as opposed to nil, a player "owns" the tile.

- **Is the AI still deciding which tile it should choose?** This check has more to do with dramatic effect than with performance. The algorithm will be simple enough that Swift should process it in the blink of an eye. Yet anticipating your opponent's next move is part of what makes tic-tac-toe fun and suspenseful. By adding an artificial timeout, you make the AI appear more human.

- **Is the game over?** This third check is self-explanatory. After a player wins or the game is tied, tapping a tile should have no effect. The tiles will remain disabled until the player taps the Reset button.

If the answer to all three questions is yes, the code proceeds to fill the selected tile with an image. The setImageForSpot function takes as parameters the number of a tile and the number of a player. At the top of the last code snippet is an enum called Player that will store the two player IDs. When a user chooses X or O, based on a given ID, setImageForSpot puts the appropriate image into a tile. After you've made all these changes to the view controller, save and run your code. An X should appear when you tap a tile.

Developing the Concept for an AI

The AI in this game involves more lines of code than any of the previous examples in this book. That's because you've learned a lot about Swift, and you're ready to put your knowledge to the test! Still, you might find it helpful to step back from the code and look at the big picture.

Even though tic-tac-toe is simple and well known, we'll briefly summarize the game's rules. A player makes a move by marking a tile with an X or an O. A player wins by covering three tiles in a row, in any direction, with his or her mark. In other words, a smart AI is one that covers three tiles before its human opponent. Specifically, there are five steps the algorithm must take, based on five things the computer player needs to "think about" before each turn:

1. "Do I have one more tile left to win in any direction? If yes, I should fill it."

2. "Does my human opponent have one more tile left to win? If so, I should block it."

3. "I should take the center tile."

4. "I'll take one of the corner tiles."

5. "I'm all out of options, so I'll take a middle tile."

To make the AI more sophisticated, you could insert an extra process between steps 3 and 4. The process, known as "blocking an opponent's fork," has to do with forcing your rival to make a defensive move. You can also make the AI guard against the human player's attempt to "fork." For simplicity's sake, we'll skip this step and focus only on the five processes listed previously. Besides, keep in mind that an AI algorithm should not be perfect. Players will become frustrated and lose interest in the game if they're never able to defeat the computer.

Managing the Game State

There's one more bit of housekeeping to attend to before you can implement the AI algorithm: You need to keep track of the overall game state. This entails tracking when the game ends and issuing an alert to say who won. Call a method named checkForWin after the imageClicked function that you created in the previous section:

```
func imageClicked(reco: UITapGestureRecognizer) {
// Other code in this method is left out for brevity
    checkForWin()
}
```

Running your code at this point will cause an error because checkForWin doesn't exist yet, but you'll create it shortly.

The checkForWin method scans the game board for winning tile combinations:

```
func checkForWin(){
    var whoWon = ["I":0,"you":1]
    for (key,value) in whoWon {
        var triggerWin:Bool = false
        if((plays[6] == value && plays[7] == value &&
            plays[8] == value)) {
              triggerWin = true
        }

        if((plays[3] == value && plays[4] == value &&
            plays[5] == value)) {
                triggerWin = true
        }
```

```
        if((plays[0] == value && plays[1] == value &&
            plays[2] == value)) {
                triggerWin = true
        }

        if((plays[6] == value && plays[3] == value &&
            plays[0] == value)) {
                triggerWin = true
        }

        if((plays[7] == value && plays[4] == value &&
            plays[1] == value)) {
                triggerWin = true
        }

        if((plays[8] == value && plays[5] == value &&
            plays[2] == value)) {
                triggerWin = true
        }

        if((plays[6] == value && plays[4] == value &&
            plays[2] == value)) {
                triggerWin = true
        }

        if((plays[8] == value && plays[4] == value &&
            plays[0] == value)) {
                triggerWin = true
        }

        if (triggerWin){
            userMessage.hidden = false
            userMessage.text = "Looks like \(key) won!"
            resetBtn.hidden = false;
            done = true;
        }
    }
}
```

Here's what happens: The method begins with the definition of a variable called whoWon. The dictionary relates a player's number, a unique ID, to a noun describing the player. Using this dictionary, you iterate exactly twice through the plays array. You may recall that plays is a two-dimensional array of integers. It contains the positions of tiles as numbers. Each number points to the ID of the player who owns the tile. In this case, you can list all winning combos because there are only a few of them: variations of a horizontal row, a vertical row, or a diagonal row. If the player's ID correlates to the tile positions of a winning combo, you have a winner! You show the `userMessage` label by switching its hidden attribute to `false`. You fill the label with victory text and display the Reset button. Finally, you set `done` to `true` to let the player know the game is finished and stop him or her from tapping other buttons.

Implementing the AI Logic

Now that you've added logic for detecting when a player wins or loses, you can make the computer player strive to achieve a victory. This concerns steps 1 and 2 of the algorithm outlined earlier: The AI should move in for the kill, so to speak, if it has two tiles in a row, and it should block the human player if the human has two tiles in a row. To start processing the AI's turn in the game, you call a new method named `aiTurn`. You place the new method calls at the bottom of the `imageClicked` function:

```
func imageClicked(reco: UITapGestureRecognizer) {
    var imageViewTapped = reco.view as UIImageView

    if plays[imageViewTapped.tag] == nil && !aiDeciding && !done {
        setImageForSpot(imageViewTapped.tag, player:.UserPlayer)
        checkForWin()
        aiTurn()
    }
}
```

A lot of logic occurs inside `aiTurn`. To make things easier to digest, we'll divide the method into two parts and focus only on the first part in this section. The following code marks the official start of the AI implementation. If you try to compile it right away, you'll notice several errors. That's because the code includes functions you haven't written yet. Don't worry! The compiler will pass your game with flying colors after you create the missing pieces.

Here is how the AI decides where it should play:

```
func aiTurn() {
  if done {
     return
  }

  aiDeciding = true
  //We (the computer) have two in a row
  if let result = rowCheck(value: 0){
    println("comp has two in a row")
    var whereToPlayResult = whereToPlay(result[0], pattern: result[1])
    if !isOccupied(whereToPlayResult) {
      setImageForSpot(whereToPlayResult, player: .ComputerPlayer)
      aiDeciding = false
      checkForWin()
      return
    }
  }
}
```

```
  //They (the player) have two in a row
  if let result = rowCheck(value: 1) {
    var whereToPlayResult = whereToPlay(result[0], pattern: result[1])
    if !isOccupied(whereToPlayResult) {
      setImageForSpot(whereToPlayResult, player: .ComputerPlayer)
      aiDeciding = false
      checkForWin()
      return
    }

    //Is center available?
  }

  if !isOccupied(4) {
    setImageForSpot(4, player: .ComputerPlayer)
    aiDeciding = false
    checkForWin()
    return
  }

  if let cornerAvailable = firstAvailable(isCorner: true){
    setImageForSpot(cornerAvailable, player: .ComputerPlayer)
    aiDeciding = false
    checkForWin()
    return
  }

  if let sideAvailable = firstAvailable(isCorner: false){
    setImageForSpot(sideAvailable, player: .ComputerPlayer)
    aiDeciding = false
    checkForWin()
    return
  }

  userMessage.hidden = false
  userMessage.text = "Looks like it was a tie!"

  reset()

  println(rowCheck(value: 0))
  println(rowCheck(value: 1))

  aiDeciding = false
}
```

The method first checks the game state. If done is true, the game is finished, and the AI has nothing left to do. In this case, a return statement skips the rest of AI logic. If the game isn't finished, the function proceeds to set `aiDeciding` to `true`. It doesn't set the variable back to `false` until the computer player has finished picking a tile. You may recall from earlier in this chapter that `imageClicked` uses `aiDeciding` to make the human player wait his or her turn while the computer is making a move.

Finding Victory Conditions

The `if` statements in `aiTurn` are where the bulk of the logic takes place. They determine whether either player has two tiles in a row. While the steps for each check are basically the same, we'll focus on the first one: the check to see whether a computer player is one tile away from a win. To answer this question, you can build a method called `rowCheck` and a series of short, related functions:

```
func rowCheck(#value:Int) -> [String]?{
    var acceptableFinds = ["011","110","101"]
    var findFuncs = [checkTop,checkBottom,checkLeft,checkRight,
        checkMiddleAcross,checkMiddleDown,
        checkDiagLeftRight,checkDiagRightLeft]
    var algorithmResults = findFuncs[0](value: value)

    for algorithm in findFuncs {
        var algorithmResults = algorithm(value: value)
        println(algorithmResults)
        var findPattern = find(acceptableFinds,algorithmResults[1])
        println(acceptableFinds)
        if findPattern != nil {
            return algorithmResults
        }
    }
    return nil
}
```

First, take note of the data types that `rowCheck` receives and gives back. It accepts an integer representing a player's ID, which can be `1` or `0`. You use this information to search for tiles that belong to a player—in this case, the computer player. If a match is found, you return a pattern indicating which type of match exists. A `011` match, for example, means the leftmost tile is blank, and the two tiles to the right are marked. A `110` match means exactly the opposite. If no match exists, the method returns `nil`. Because the return type can vary, you have a great excuse to use an optional.

The `acceptableFinds` array describes which patterns indicate a match. The `findFuncs` array is closely related. It contains functions that check for certain types of matches. The concept of storing methods in an array may sound confusing if you're not used to functional programming. Remember that functions are *first-class members* in Swift, which means they can be passed as arguments to other functions. To see exactly how `rowCheck` uses `findFuncs`, look at how you define all the methods included in the array:

```
func checkBottom(#value:Int) -> [String]{
    return ["bottom",checkFor(value, inList: [6,7,8])]
}
func checkMiddleAcross(#value:Int) -> [String]{
    return ["middleHorz",checkFor(value, inList: [3,4,5])]
}
func checkTop(#value:Int) -> [String]{
    return ["top",checkFor(value, inList: [0,1,2])]
}
func checkLeft(#value:Int) -> [String]{
    return ["left",checkFor(value, inList: [0,3,6])]
}
func checkMiddleDown(#value:Int) -> [String]{
    return ["middleVert",checkFor(value, inList: [1,4,7])]
}
func checkRight(#value:Int) ->  [String]{
    return ["right",checkFor(value, inList: [2,5,8])]
}
func checkDiagLeftRight(#value:Int) ->  [String]{
    return ["diagRightLeft",checkFor(value, inList: [2,4,6])]
}
func checkDiagRightLeft(#value:Int) ->  [String]{
    return ["diagLeftRight",checkFor(value, inList: [0,4,8])]
}
```

Notice the logic that these checks have in common. Given a player's ID as an integer, they check certain types of winning conditions. Each one returns an array of two elements, both of which are strings. The first string describes a type of match in easy-to-read human terms. The second string consists of three numbers. It represents the type of tile pattern, if any, that the algorithm found. This three-number string results from the checkFor method, which you define like this:

```
func checkFor(value:Int, inList:[Int]) -> String {
    var conclusion = ""
    for cell in inList {
        if plays[cell] == value {
            conclusion += "1"
        }else{
            conclusion += "0"
        }
    }
    return conclusion
}
```

To understand how checkFor comes into play, take a look at the checkTop method. The tile numbers 0, 1, and 2 represent the top row of the game board. The checkTop method passes to checkFor an array made up of these numbers. Looping through the given integers, checkFor finds out whether the corresponding tiles belong to the computer player. The `conclusion` variable will be a three-number string if a match is found and an empty string if no match exists.

Now that you've explored `findFuncs`, refer to the place in `rowCheck` where you loop through the array:

```
var findFuncs = [checkTop,checkBottom,checkLeft,checkRight,
            checkMiddleAcross,checkMiddleDown,
            checkDiagLeftRight,checkDiagRightLeft]
for algorithm in findFuncs {
    var algorithmResults = algorithm(value: value)
    var findPattern = find(acceptableFinds,algorithmResults[1])
    if findPattern != nil {
        return algorithmResults
    }
}
```

The `algorithm` in the `for` statement references each of the elements in `findFuncs`. In the loop's first iteration, calling `algorithm()` is the same as calling `checkTop()`. In the second pass-through, `algorithm()` is the same as `checkBottom()`. This pattern continues until the loop reaches the end of the array. You know, then, that `algorithmResults` will always contain a string made up of nothing or three numbers. Remember from our definition of `rowCheck` that `acceptableFinds` features a list of winning conditions. If `algorithmResults` isn't empty, and it matches an element in `acceptableFinds`, you've identified a winning tile. The machine has outsmarted the human. It's a sad day for humankind, but a good achievement for you as a Swift programmer.

Moving In for the Win

By using `rowCheck` and a few related functions, you've taught the AI how to scan the game board for a winning tile. The next step is teaching it how to take action, marking a tile to secure victory. The `rowCheck` method includes many moving parts, so to speak. If you're not entirely sure how it works, consider reviewing the previous sections before moving forward. When you're ready to continue, step back and look at `rowCheck` in the context of `aiTurn`:

```
if let result = rowCheck(value: 0){
    println("computer has two in a row")
    var whereToPlayResult = whereToPlay(result[0], pattern: result[1])
    if !isOccupied(whereToPlayResult) {
        setImageForSpot(whereToPlayResult, player: .ComputerPlayer)
        aiDeciding = false
        checkForWin()
        return
    }
}
```

You've defined all but two methods in the block of code: `whereToPlay` and `isOccupied`. You pass to `whereToPlay` a pattern that's only one tile away from triggering a victory. The function uses this pattern to figure out the position of the remaining tile:

```
func whereToPlay(location:String,pattern:String) -> Int {
        var leftPattern = "011"
        var rightPattern = "110"
        var middlePattern = "101"
        switch location {
            case "top":
                if pattern == leftPattern {
                    return 0
                }else if pattern == rightPattern{
                    return 2
                }else{
                    return 1
                }
            case "bottom":
                if pattern == leftPattern {
                    return 6
                }else if pattern == rightPattern{
                    return 8
                }else{
                    return 7
                }
            case "left":
                if pattern == leftPattern {
                    return 0
                }else if pattern == rightPattern{
                    return 6
                }else{
                    return 3
                }
            case "right":
                if pattern == leftPattern {
                    return 2
                }else if pattern == rightPattern{
                    return 8
                }else{
                    return 5
                }
            case "middleVert":
                if pattern == leftPattern {
                    return 1
                }else if pattern == rightPattern{
                    return 7
                }else{
```

```
                return 4
            }
        case "middleHorz":
            if pattern == leftPattern {
                return 3
            }else if pattern == rightPattern{
                return 5
            }else{
                return 4
            }
        case "diagLeftRight":
            if pattern == leftPattern {
                return 0
            }else if pattern == rightPattern{
                return 8
            }else{
                return 4
            }
        case "diagRightLeft":
            if pattern == leftPattern {
                return 2
            }else if pattern == rightPattern{
                return 6
            }else{
                return 4
            }

        default:
        return 4
    }
}
```

Now that you've defined `whereToPlay`, take another look at the first `if` statement in `aiTurn`. You know that `whereToPlayResult` will store an integer representing a tile position. There's only one issue: You need to make sure that the human player doesn't already "own" it. If the tile is taken, the computer can't move forward and seize it. That's where `isOccupied` comes into play:

```
func isOccupied(spot:Int) -> Bool {
    println("occupied \(spot)")
    if plays[spot] != nil {
        return true
    }
    return false
}
```

The method performs a check of plays to see whether a player has claimed a spot on the game board. Remember that plays is a two-dimensional array full of integer pairs. When a player claims a tile, plays keeps track of the tile's position, along with the player's ID.

As an aside, notice that isOccupied is simple and brief—only seven lines long. Couldn't you delete it and check plays directly within aiTurn? This is partially a matter of style, but storing the logic in a function has advantages. Imagine that in the future, you change the criteria for tiles being occupied. The new logic involves checking two arrays instead of one. If the logic is *abstracted* into the isOccupied function, you can make a single edit, and your app should work correctly. On the other hand, if you copy and paste if statements, you'll probably spend extra time editing and debugging. Think carefully about abstraction as you venture into building bigger apps with Swift.

Now let's refer to aiTurn to see how isOccupied fits into the big picture. If the method returns false, the AI player is free at last to mark a tile. The app will update the UI and then indicate that the computer has made up its mind. Finally, you call checkForWin to update the game state. In this case, the function always reveals a message stating that the computer has won. Here's the isOccupied method in context:

```
if !isOccupied(whereToPlayResult) {
    setImageForSpot(whereToPlayResult, player: .ComputerPlayer)
    aiDeciding = false
    checkForWin()
    return
}
```

Defending the AI's Turf and Stealing Center Stage

The computer now knows how to take action when it's one tile away from a win. In the five-step outline for the AI, the second priority was finding and blocking a human player's winning tile; basically, the AI wants to defend its turf. The methods from step 1 are generic enough that you can reuse them to defend the AI's turf in step 2. The only difference is that you have to pass the human player ID instead of the computer ID to rowCheck and setImageForSpot:

```
// The player has two in a row
if let result = rowCheck(value: 1) {
    var whereToPlayResult = whereToPlay(result[0], pattern: result[1])
    if !isOccupied(whereToPlayResult) {
        setImageForSpot(whereToPlayResult, player: .UserPlayer)
        aiDeciding = false
        checkForWin()
        return
    }
}
```

With the first two if statements in aiTurn, the AI can move in for a victory and defend itself against a human's near-victory. If no such scenarios exist on the game board, the computer has to pick a different course of action. That's when the algorithm arrives at step 3: choosing the center tile. If the size of the board varied, you might have to compute the position of the center tile. Fortunately, you know the board consists of nine tiles. Counting from zero, left to right and top to bottom, the fourth tile is in the center. To select the tile, you pass its position to isOccupied and setImageForSpot:

```
//Is center available?
if !isOccupied(4) {
    setImageForSpot(4, player: .ComputerPlayer)
    aiDeciding = false
    checkForWin()
    return
}
```

Taking Sides

You're almost done creating an AI in Swift. If the computer player can't seize a victory, block the opponent's win, or take a center tile, it has only two options. It tries step 4, claiming a corner tile. If all corners are taken, it falls back to its last resort, marking a middle tile. Steps 4 and 5 are similar in terms of logic:

```
func firstAvailable(#isCorner:Bool) -> Int? {
    var spots = isCorner ? [0,2,6,8] : [1,3,5,7]
    for spot in spots {
        println("checking \(spot)")
        if !isOccupied(spot) {
            println("not occupied \(spot)")
            return spot
        }
    }
    return nil
}
```

The firstAvailable method loops through an array of tile positions and returns the first open tile. The array contents differ, depending on which tiles you care about. Corners occupy tiles 0, 2, 6, and 8. Side tiles take up positions 1, 3, 5, and 7. The firstAvailable method returns an integer if a match exists or nil if all tiles are taken.

When It's a Draw

The if statements in aiTurn account for every possible move available to the AI. The statements also include a return so that if a block executes, the following if blocks won't be reached. These facts tell you that the compiler won't reach the bottom of aiTurn unless all tiles are taken and neither player has won. In other words, you know that the game has ended in a tie. Here's how you add logic to the end of aiTurn to handle this scenario:

```
userMessage.hidden = false
userMessage.text = "Looks like it was a tie!"
reset()
```

After the AI outsmarts the user, the human player will be itching to jump back into the game. You can oblige him or her by defining a `reset` function that will clear the board:

```
func reset() {
    plays = [:]
    ticTacImage1.image = nil
    ticTacImage2.image = nil
    ticTacImage3.image = nil
    ticTacImage4.image = nil
    ticTacImage5.image = nil
    ticTacImage6.image = nil
    ticTacImage7.image = nil
    ticTacImage8.image = nil
    ticTacImage9.image = nil
}
@IBAction func resetBtnClicked(sender : UIButton) {
    done = false
    resetBtn.hidden = true
    userMessage.hidden = true
    reset()
}
```

You're done! This marks the end of implementing the AI. Take a moment to read over your code and make sure it includes all the methods discussed in this chapter. When you're ready, click the Play button in Xcode to preview the finished product. Figure 5.4 shows a glimpse.

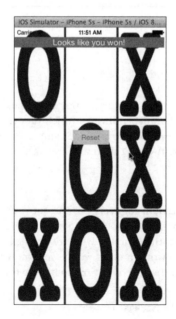

Figure 5.4   The game in action.

For an extra challenge, try enhancing tic-tac-toe:

- Add steps to the algorithm so that the computer player "forks" and anticipates the human player's "fork."
- Enhance the UI by designing graphics of your own.
- Create a separate class outside the `viewController` for methods related to the AI.

Summary

In this chapter you have learned how to dissect and model a problem by using Swift. First, you learned how to set up a full-fledged Xcode project. We walked through the steps for building UI elements and linking them to your code. Working with predefined classes like `viewController` gave you a glimpse into how bigger apps are organized. Besides learning about projects in Xcode, you applied key features of the Swift language. In the tic-tac-toe exercise you used classes, enumerators, and functions. The features let you reuse code instead of rewriting it, which saved time and reduced the potential for bugs. You applied `for`, `if`, and `switch` statements to control the game's logic flow.

6

Reusable Code: Closures

Closures in Swift have their own special syntax. When relating closures to Objective-C, you can think of closures as self-contained blocks of functionality. When you use them, you often directly replace an Objective-C block. You use them for things like creating a callback after a URL has been fetched from a server or calling a function when an animation is done. You use them for things like sorting, when you need to pass a special sort function.

What Are Closures?

Closures are a familiar concept in many languages. Closures can be created when an environment is enclosed in a referencing unit of scope. We often say "a function within another function" when we're talking about closures. But the real closure itself happens *because* you put a function within another function. When you put that function within the other function, the inner function has a reference to the outer function.

In languages other than Swift, closures are not often defined as a special syntactic structure. This is usually what makes them a difficult concept to grasp. For example, in JavaScript, you can create a closure by just putting one function inside another. The inner function will have access to all the local variables of the outer function. If the outer function returns the inner function, you now have a permanent reference to the inner function, which still has access to the outer function's local variables. This works in Swift as well.

In short, closures are functions that refer to independent variables. Functions defined in a closure remember the environment in which they were created—even after everything has run. This is interesting because local variables are usually trashed after a function has run.

Things get really interesting when you realize that operators in Swift are implemented as functions themselves. Take, for example, the less-than sign ($<$). It takes two parameters: a left-hand parameter and a right-hand parameter. So you see, closures can be written in extremely simple and concise ways.

Closures in Other Languages

It may be helpful to see closures in a broader context. A closure itself is relatively the same in all languages. However, Swift provides extra-special syntax for closures, which makes their implementation a bit different. In JavaScript you can create a closure by writing a function within another function. That inner function does not exist outside the outer function and therefore is "enclosed" (hence the name *closure*) in the outer function. The outer function can then return the inner function and make it available to all. Now the outer function has finished running, and all of its local variables should be dumped. But they aren't because the inner function is now available globally and still has references to the outer function's local variables. Let's look at some code to see how this works. This is code written in JavaScript, not Swift:

```javascript
function nameClosure() {
    var name = "Skip Tastic"
    function sayYourName() {
        console.log(name);
    }
    return sayYourName;
}
var yourName = nameClosure()
yourName()
```

When `nameClosure` is called, it returns `sayYourName` and therefore is the inner function itself. Now you have a reference to the inner function `sayYourName`. The inner function has a reference to the local variable name even though `init` has been called and passed. So when you call the variable you set as `yourName`, you get the console to log the local variable. This is actually similar to summoning the dead. Try this example:

1. Open Google Chrome.

2. On any tab, right-click the screen and click Inspect Element.

3. When the developer tools open, choose the Console tab, which is like a dumbed-down JavaScript playground.

4. Type in the previous JavaScript code.

You could write this same example in Swift. Here's how:

```swift
func nameClosure() -> () -> () {
    var name = "Skip Tastic"
    func sayYourName() {
        println(name)
    }
    return sayYourName
}
var yourName = nameClosure()
yourName()
```

You can see that this code is almost exactly the same as the JavaScript code. One change is that you replace `function` with `func`. In Swift, you have to be a little more specific if you are going to return a function. You need to tell Swift that this function returns its own function. Because functions on their own have types, you need to return a function that returns `Void`. The way you express a function that returns nothing or `Void` is to say that the function returns an empty tuple, which is essentially void. So the type of return value of `nameClosure` is `()->()`. This is because `sayYourName` does not return anything.

In the end, you will see that the Swift code prints out the result of the local variable, as promised. This is good because after you understand closures, you can apply them to any language. Swift happens to be a great place to learn closures, and the excitement doesn't stop with what you've seen so far. In fact, it goes so much farther that I think your mind will be blown by the end of the chapter.

How Closures Work and Why They're Awesome

Swift defines a closure syntax that is different from the regular function syntax. This syntax allows you to do a couple things: It allows you to infer the type of the object from the context, and it allows you to return a value without actually writing `return`. There are several different ways to write closures in Swift, and some of them take very little code. If you are used to replacing or rewriting Objective-C syntax, you may have seen blocks as the last parameter of a function. Swift allows you to write closures outside functions when they are the last parameters. This gives you a nice clean-looking syntax.

Let's take a look at the `sort` function in Swift. For this example, you are going to pass two parameters to the `sort` function. The first is an `inout` parameter of the array you would like to sort. The second parameter is the function you would like to use to sort the array. The function must take two `Strings` as parameters and return a `Bool`. You will check whether each string is less than the other string in order to sort the string alphabetically. (When you compare two strings with a less-than or greater-than operator, Swift sorts strings alphabetically either in a reverse or forward direction.) The following code sorts the array alphabetically:

```
var names = ["john","sam","zed","bob","harry","noa"]
func alphabetical(s1:String,s2:String) -> Bool {
    return s1 < s2
}
sort(&names,alphabetical)
```

The `sort` function takes each of the strings in the array, one at a time, and compares them to each other by running them through the function. Notice that there is a global function to do the sorting. You pass this function into `sort`. We talked previously about the type of a function. In this case, the function is of type `(s1: String, s2: String) -> Bool`. You can find this out by three-finger-clicking the function name. If you three-finger-click the `sort` function, you see what it needs in order to work: `func sort<T>(inout array: [T], predicate: (T, T) -> Bool)`. This syntax may look a little foreign at this point because we haven't covered anything like it. This is the syntax for generics, which you'll learn about Chapter 9,

"Becoming Flexible with Generics." You can think of the `T` as standing for anything you want. It could be a `String`, an `Int`, a car, a cat, or whatever. So the `sort` function takes an `inout` array with any type in it. It also takes a function/closure that has two parameters of the same type and then returns a `Bool`. Note that `T` is different from `AnyObject`. Whereas `AnyObject` can be a `String` or an `Int`, `T` must be of one type. Using `T` is like saying you don't know the type yet but we will choose it later. Using `AnyObject` allows you to have a mix of a bunch of types together.

The Closure Syntax

You can rewrite that last alphabetical function to be an inline closure. It would look like this:

```
var alphabetical = {(s1:String, s2:String) -> Bool in s1 < s2}
```

You remove the `func` keyword and the name of the function. You put the whole thing in some curly brackets and put the actual content after the word in and remove the keyword `return`. The closure knows that it should return stuff. The closure by itself doesn't do much. You need to either save it to a variable or pass it directly into the `sort` function. Notice how it still matches the signature of the previous function you used. It takes two `Strings` and returns a `Boolean`. Now you can pass this into the `sort` function:

```
sort(&names,{(s1:String, s2:String) -> Bool in s1 < s2})
```

What is so cool about this is that you can define a whole reusable functionality within the `sort` function itself. The `sort` function does not have to go anywhere else to get the closure it will use to sort the array.

Inferring Using Context

The `sort` function must take an array and a function with a specific signature. In the example we've been working with, the function must take two parameters that are `Strings`. You cannot use any other types in this case. You and I know this, and Swift does, too. You can shorten the closure syntax because you know that `s1` and `s2` are `Strings`. You can also shorten the closure because you know that the return type must be a `Bool`. Who the heck needs to write a return type when you already know it must be a `Bool`? Here is a shorter closure you can pass to the `sort` function:

```
sort(&names,{s1, s2 in s1 < s2})
```

Now you have a much shorter, easier closure.

Let's review what's happened so far: You first took a regular old function and passed it to the `sort`. Then you rewrote the function as a closure and passed it to the `sort`. Then you realized you didn't need to do any typing because Swift can infer types from the context. So you rewrote the closure by removing the types and parentheses. Notice that you never had to write the `return` keyword because it is also inferred.

Arguments Have a Shorthand, Too

As it turns out, you don't even have to declare s1 and s2 as the parameters. You can use a special syntax to get the *n*th parameter. You can write $0 to get the first parameter and $1 to get the second parameter and so on. Now the closure gets even shorter because you no longer need to declare the names of parameters. You can pass the closure to sort like so:

```
sort(&names,{$0 < $1})
```

You are able to write this because of all the things mentioned before plus the fact that you don't have to declare parameters if you use a special argument shorthand. Why declare something that does not need to be declared? You don't need the return keyword, and you don't need to declare a type for the parameters because it is inferred. This closure does return a Bool because it is comparing two things together. This is an extremely flexible closure because it does not declare any types. If your array contained Ints, Doubles, Floats, or your own custom type, then this closure would still work just fine.

Sorting a Custom Car Class

To sort a custom class, you need the class to inherit two protocols: Comparable and Equatable. Here's how you could define a short Car class that just has a name property:

```
class Car:Comparable,Equatable {
    var name:String

    init(name:String) {
        self.name = name
    }
}
```

To implement Comparable and Equatable, you must teach Swift how to compare two cars. Because the name of the car is a String, you can use the name. You need to write global functions that define the <, >, <=, >=, and == signs. One caveat is that you should not write these functions within the Car class; rather, you should write them globally. Here's an example of how to do that:

```
func ==(lhs: Car, rhs: Car) -> Bool{
    return lhs.name == rhs.name
}
func <=(lhs: Car, rhs: Car) -> Bool{
    return lhs.name <= rhs.name
}
func >=(lhs: Car, rhs: Car) -> Bool{
    return lhs.name >= rhs.name
}
func >(lhs: Car, rhs: Car) -> Bool{
    return lhs.name > rhs.name
}
```

```
func <(lhs: Car, rhs: Car) -> Bool {
    return lhs.name < rhs.name
}
```

Here you are naming the functions with the signs they represent. Notice that you could redefine these functions for comparison of other classes.

Finally, you can create a cars array and sort it, like this:

```
var cars = [Car(name:"Ford"),Car(name:"Mercedes")]
sort(&cars,{$0 < $1})
cars
```

Here you create two cars in an array of cars. Then you sort the array, which uses the comparison functions to compare the two cars. If you ever needed to compare other types of classes, you could rewrite the > and < functions to accommodate those other types. Remember that you can have two functions with the same name as long as the method is different in some way. That is what makes it legit to make multiple less-than functions. Also note that you could create the comparison functions on a protocol or base class. This would give you the option of comparing multiple classes with the same comparison. It's a win–win for everybody. Here is our shortest closure yet:

```
sort(&names,<)
```

Okay, now this is impressive. I would say that this is the ultimate in refactoring.

Closures Are Reference Types

Chapter 4, "Structuring Code: Enums, Structs, and Classes," talks about reference types and value types. It talks about the difference between things being copied versus being referenced when they are passed around. If you think about it, it makes a lot of sense for closures to be reference types rather than value types. Closures capture values in their context. If a closure were copied every time it was passed around, it would lose context that it has access to. In other words, it would lose access to those local variables. Here's an example:

```
func increment(n:Int)-> ()->Int {
    var i = 0
    var incrementByN = {
        () -> Int in
        i += n
        return i
    }
    return incrementByN
}
var inner = increment(4)
inner() //4
inner() //8
inner() //12
```

This example changes things up a little bit. In the end, you use the inner closure that holds a reference to i, incrementByN, to increment that local variable i by 4. The main point is that the inner closure has a reference to that local variable after the function has returned and the closure you use is passed by reference, which makes the number increment each time.

Automatic Reference Counting

Now is a good time to talk about Automatic Reference Counting, otherwise known as ARC. If you are an Objective-C programmer, then you know all about ARC. If you were one of the first iPhone programmers, you know that you used to have to do your own reference counting. You will be happy to know that for the most part, you can let Swift worry about the management of memory.

When you create instances of classes, those classes exist by reference. When those instances are no longer needed, Swift cleans them up for you.

ARC works by keeping track of the instances of classes that you create and where those instances are referenced. Every time you create a new instance of a class, ARC finds some free memory available where you can place the new instance. You don't need to worry about how this works; just know that it works. (Of course, those details are available to you if you feel like diving in; go to https://developer.apple.com/library/ios/documentation/swift/conceptual/swift_programming_language/AutomaticReferenceCounting.html.) When you no longer need that instance of the class, ARC takes back that memory it gave you and deallocates your instance. If Swift were not smart and accidentally deallocated an instance you were still using, then you would no longer be able to access your class and all its properties.

To tell Swift "I'm using this, don't deallocate it," you assign that class reference to a variable or constant. When you do this, you are creating a strong reference. Swift won't deallocate that memory associated with your class instance because you said you needed it. Imagine Rose in *Titanic*, saying she would "never let go." Well that's a bad example because eventually Rose did let go. But it's actually a good example because Rose only let go when she was sure Jack was dead and gone. Swift will not allow it to be deallocated as long as the strong reference remains. You can deallocate that instance by assigning it to nil. Take a look at this example, using the Car class from earlier:

```
var c1 = Car(name: "Ford")
```

Here you create a new instance of the Car class. ARC allocates some memory for a new instance of Car. You have one instance of the Car class allocated: Let's reference c1 a couple more time.

```
var c2 = c1
var c3 = c2
```

Now you have three references to the one instance of the Car class. But these are not just any references; they are three strong references. For Swift to deallocate the single instance of Car, you need to assign all three of these references to nil. If you were to assign two out of three to nil, the instance would remain in memory because it would be still in use. You can assign c1 and c2 to nil:

```
c1 = nil
c2 = nil
```

You now have one reference of the `Car` class still out there. ARC is counting this instance of the `Car` class, so it remains allocated in memory. You can assign `c3` to `nil` to completely remove all references to the instance of the car:

```
c3 = nil
```

Now the single instance of `Car` is deallocated because all three references have been unreferenced by being set to `nil`. By the way, if you create an optional property, that property is initialized with `nil` and not any instance of a class. You can rewrite the `Car` class a tad and add a new class for a driver as well:

```
class Driver {
    var car:Car?
}
class Car {
    var name:String
    var driver:Driver?
    init(name:String) {
        self.name = name
    }
}
```

When you create a new `Car` instance, `driver` is created and set to `nil`.

Strong Reference Cycles

By letting ARC do its thing, you can pretty much sit back and relax as ARC allocates and deallocates memory when it is needed. However, there are situations when Rose really never lets go—when you create a permanent bond between two classes. Consider the new `Car` and `Driver` classes. Notice that when you create a new `Driver` and new `Car`, your driver's car will be `nil` and your car's driver will be `nil`. You can see what I mean when I create a new car and driver:

```
var car = Car(name: "Ford")
var driver = Driver()
```

Now you have a new `car` and new `driver` that ARC has reference counted. `driver` has a car that is `nil`, and car has a driver that is `nil`. Now you can assign car's `driver` to car and driver's `car` to car:

```
car.driver = driver
driver.car = car
```

You have now created a permanent strong reference between those two instances that can never be resolved. If you set `car` to `nil` and `driver` to `nil`, neither will ever be deallocated. The way you can tell is by using the special `deinit` function. This function is called when the class is deinitialized. You can add it to both the `Car` and `Driver` classes. To see `deinit` in action, you must run your code in a project instead of in the playground. You can start a new game project and create your `Car` and `Driver` classes directly in `ViewController.swift`. Then in `viewDidLoad`, you can initialize and deinitialize your `car` and `driver` classes:

```
class Car {
    var driver:Driver?
    init() {
        println("INITTING Car")
    }
    deinit {
        println("DEINITTING Car")
    }
}
class Driver {
    var car:Car?
    init() {
        println("INITTING Driver")
    }
    deinit {
        println("DEINITTING Driver")
    }
}
```

Now in your `didLoadView` function, you can test `init` and `deinit` by creating an optional `car` then setting it to `nil`. When you create the `car`, the `init` method runs. Then setting the `car` to `nil` calls the `deinit` method. You must set the `car` to be optional so that you can later send it to `nil`:

```
override func viewDidLoad() {
    super.viewDidLoad()
    var car:Car? = Car()
    car = nil
}
```

Now when you run this, you see that the `car` was first initialized and then deinitialized. Now let's get back to the strong reference cycle. If you create a new `driver` and the new `car` and assign the `car`'s `driver` to the new `driver` and vice versa, if you then try to set the `car` and the `driver` to `nil`, you see that neither gets deinitialized:

```
override func viewDidLoad() {
    super.viewDidLoad()
    var car:Car? = Car()
    var driver:Driver? = Driver()
    car!.driver = driver
    driver!.car = car
    car = nil
    driver = nil
}
```

You have created a strong reference cycle and a memory leak. In this case, `car` and `driver` will never be deallocated.

unowned **Versus** weak

Swift provides a solution for strong reference cycles by allowing you to use the keyword weak or the keyword unowned. You use the keyword weak when it is possible for your reference to have no value at some point. If this isn't the case, then you use unowned.

The weak Keyword

A weak reference does not keep a stronghold to the instance that it refers to. When you assign a reference as weak, you are saying that it may at some point have "no value." Therefore, you must assign a weak reference as an optional. It is possible that a weak reference may be deallocated before you are done with it. ARC automatically sets weak references to nil when they are deallocated. You can then easily check this with an if statement.

To see how this works, you can rewrite the car and driver example and set one of the variables to weak. You don't need to set both to weak, just one, because when there are no more strong references to the car or driver, it will be deallocated. The only change you really need to make is either in the car or driver class. You just need to mark the variable as weak in one of the classes. For now, do this in the driver class. Edit your driver class to look like this (and notice I am only adding one word here).

Run the code, and you'll see that car and driver both get initialized and deinitialized:

```
//INITTING Car
//INITTING Driver
//DEINITTING Car
//DEINITTING Driver
```

The unowned Keyword

Instead of using weak, you can use unowned. The big difference between unowned and weak is that unowned is assumed to always have a value. Therefore, it does not need to be an optional. You have to be super-duper careful when using unowned because, whereas weak sets your variable to nil after it's been deallocated, unowned does not. If you try to reference an unowned variable after it's been deallocated, your program will reliably crash. Therefore, you want to use unowned only when you are absolutely positive it will always have a value. Here's how you can rewrite the driver class to use unowned instead of weak:

```
class Driver {
    unowned var car:Car
    init(car:Car) {
        self.car = car
        println("INITTING Driver")
    }
    deinit {
        println("DEINITTING Driver")
    }
}
```

You must now add an initializer for `driver` because `car` is no longer an optional. You also have to change `viewDidLoad` because you are no longer dealing with an optional car. Update your code like so:

```
override func viewDidLoad() {
    super.viewDidLoad()
    var car:Car? = Car()
    var driver = Driver(car: car!)
    car!.driver = driver
    driver.car = car!
    car = nil
}
```

When you run this code, notice that you get the same result. `car` and the `driver` are both deinitialized properly. Why does this work now, when it didn't work before? Well, remember that when you have a strong reference, ARC cannot deallocate the instance. When you have a strong reference cycle (when you don't use `weak` or `unowned`), it goes in both directions. `car` strongly references `driver`, and `driver` strongly references `car` (see Figure 6.1). When you mark one of the references as weak, you get rid of that strong reference that was going bidirectionally. The same goes for unowned: Swift is no longer able to have a bidirectional strong reference.

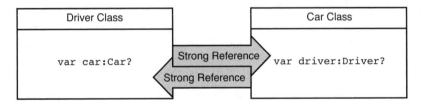

Figure 6.1   Strong references in both directions.

When you mark the `driver` of the `car` class as `weak` or you no longer have a strong reference, ARC can deallocate that instance (see Figure 6.2).

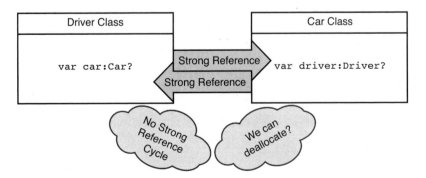

Figure 6.2   No longer fused at the hip. ARC can deallocate.

The same goes for unowned: When you mark the driver of the car class as unowned, you no longer have a strong reference, and ARC can deallocate that instance (see Figure 6.3).

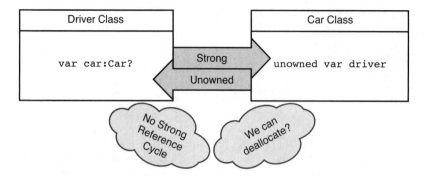

Figure 6.3   Once again not fused at the hip. ARC can deallocate.

Thus sayeth the ARC.

Strong Reference Cycles in Closures

An important point in this chapter about closures is that you can create strong reference cycles in closures. This is the bottom line: If you have a closure as a property of a class, and that closure references self, then you have a strong reference cycle. The closure can reference any property of the class. Remember that closures are referenced types, so a reference will be created.

You need to run the next example in a project. So either reopen your last project or open up a new project in Xcode. I am using a SpriteKit game setup for this project. In the view controller, you alter the car class from before. You also use a new keyword, lazy, so that you can use self within the closure. Lazy properties do not get evaluated until they are used. Therefore, by marking this closure as lazy, you know that self will exist, and we can use it. You will often use lazy when there are values that you want to use that will not be available until after initialization. You can only use values in properties that are available before initialization unless you use lazy. lazy is evaluated at runtime, if it is even used it all. If it is never used, it is never evaluated. Check out the following example:

```
class Car {
    var make:String
    var model:String
    var year:Int

    init(make:String,model:String,year:Int) {
        self.make = make
        self.model = model
        self.year = year
        println("INITTING Car")
```

```
    }

    lazy var fullName:() -> String = {
        return "\(self.year) \(self.make) \(self.model)"
    }

    deinit {
        println("DEINITTING Car")
    }
}
```

Here you have created a closure with a strong reference cycle. You can now initialize this class and attempt to deinitialize it, which will be unsuccessful because of the strong reference cycle. Because you are using SpriteKit, you can do this in the `viewDidLoad` function:

```
override func viewDidLoad() {
    super.viewDidLoad()
    var car:Car? = Car(make: "Ford", model: "Taurus", year: 1997)
    println(car!.fullName())
    car = nil
}
```

Run this code by pressing Command+R or by selecting Product > Run. You should see that everything works except the `car` is never deinitialized.

To prevent strong reference cycles for closures, you define a *capture list* when writing your closure. You create these in the same way that you create weak and unowned references for other variables. Creating a capture list allows you to capture different class instances and make sure they are no longer strongly referenced. You can mark `self` or any other class property as `weak` or `unowned` to allow ARC to deallocate instances when necessary.

To fix the `car` class so that you no longer have a strong reference cycle, you only need to add one line of code, highlighted in the following:

```
class Car {
    var make:String
    var model:String
    var year:Int

    init(make:String,model:String,year:Int) {
        self.make = make
        self.model = model
        self.year = year
        println("INITTING Car")
    }

    lazy var fullName:() -> String = {
        [unowned self] in
        return "\(self.year) \(self.make) \(self.model)"
```

```
    }

    deinit {
        println("DEINITTING Car")
    }
}
```

Now if you run this code, you will notice that the car class is properly deinitialized. You can add multiple properties to the capture list; just separate them using commas.

Trailing Closures

When you write a closure as a parameter of a function, the closure is often the last parameter. You see this often in Objective-C as well with blocks. In Objective-C, you write something like this when animating:

```
[UIView animateWithDuration:1.50 delay:0
options:(UIViewAnimationOptionCurveEaseOut|UIViewAnimationOptionBeginFromCurrentState)
animations:^{
    //do animations here.
}];
```

Notice that this function takes two blocks, and you have one block at the end. You could write the last block as a trailing closure. This means you could write the closure outside the function's closing parentheses. You could rewrite the last function in Swift like so:

```
UIView.animateWithDuration(1.50) {
    // do animations here.
}
```

Here you take advantage of the ability to write closures outside functions. Without using the trailing closure, the preceding call would look like this:

```
UIView.animateWithDuration(1.50, animations: {
    // do animations here
})
```

You don't have to write animations: explicitly with the trailing version because Swift automatically knows that animations is the last parameter and it is a closure. This makes your code cleaner because you don't have to keep track of the closing parentheses, and it also means less writing for you. Furthermore, in certain situations, you can even do away with the parentheses. If the closure is the function's only argument, then you need not include the parentheses at all. For example, say that you have a function like this that takes only one argument:

```
func gimmeAClosure(yumClosures:()->()) {
    //some good stuff goes here
}
```

Then when you call this function, you don't even need to include the parentheses at all:

```
gimmeAClosure {
    //some closure stuff
}
```

> **Note**
> This is super convenient and potentially confusing if you had never read that you can call func-tions and pass in closures without parentheses. If you ran into this syntax while examining someone's code, you may find yourself a tad confused.

Summary

In this chapter you have learned how closures work—how they "enclose" values in their context. You have learned that Swift provides specific closure syntax for writing them. Closures in the wild can be confusing if you aren't used to all the syntactic possibilities. In this chapter you have learned pretty much everything you might wind up running into.

Often when learning a new language, you find yourself trying to relate bits and pieces to other languages you already know. When converting Objective-C to Swift (which you're sure to do often), you'll notice that you can directly replace blocks with closures. When replacing them, you often have multiple syntax choices that can make your writing even shorter.

7

Subscripts and Advanced Operators

Swift is such a powerful language that it allows you to create your own new full-fledged language. You will hear people talk about writing functional Swift and writing JQuery-like Swift. It is great to have such flexibility. With Swift you can take an existing syntax and apply it to other things. For example, subscripts allow you to provide functionality to the square brackets notation. What you do with that square brackets notation is up to you. You can provide subscripts for enumerations, structures, and classes. You can use subscripts to query a class to get some sort of information back.

You probably know subscripts from arrays and dictionaries. You use subscripts to access members of an array by using the square brackets notation (for example, `myArray[5]` to get the sixth element of an array). You use the square brackets notation in dictionaries as well to access values by their key. In both arrays and dictionaries, this implementation is written using subscripts. You can prove this by looking at the Swift source code. I'll show you how to do that in a second.

With advanced operators, you have the ability to program on the bit and byte levels. Swift gives you basic operators as well as advanced operators—operators like the bitwise `AND` operator, which combines the bits of two numbers.

I combined subscripts and advanced operators in one chapter because Swift allows you to write your own custom operators. This is obviously all a part of the master plan to describe your own custom language syntax. Often it's important to define your own custom operators in your custom classes, structs, and enums. Think of the custom `Car` class you have been using in other chapters. How would you add two cars together with the standard + operator? One thing is for sure: Swift doesn't know how to add two cars together for you. You have to tell Swift how to do this. And to do that, you need to define your own custom syntax for writing Swift.

Writing Your First Subscript

To create a subscript, you use the keyword `subscript` in your class, struct, or enum. A basic subscript looks like this:

```
class Hand {
    let fingers = ["thumb","index","middle","ring","pinky"]
    subscript(i:Int) -> String{
        return fingers[i]
    }
}
let hand = Hand()
println("I had to use my \(hand[2]) finger to on the way into work today.")
```

Here you are creating a class called `Hand`, which has five fingers. You can access each finger by index. After you create a new instance `hand`, you can access the thumb by using `hand[0]`. This directly accesses the `fingers` array. You can read and write to subscripts. You can mark them as read-only or read-write. Currently the `hand/fingers` access is a read-only property. To make it writable, you have to tell Swift, like this:

```
class Hand {
    var fingers = ["thumb","index","middle","ring","pinky"]
    subscript(i:Int) -> String{
        get{
            return fingers[i]
        }
        set{
            fingers[i] = newValue
        }
    }
}
let hand = Hand()
//Not everyone calls it a pinky. Let's rename it to pinkie.
hand[4] = "pinkie"
println("I use my \(hand[4]) when I drink tea.")
```

You tell the subscript that you want it to be readable and writeable by adding the `get` and `set` properties to it. You access the finger of the hand by using the getter. You have to explicitly write a getter for this subscript because you are adding a setter as well. If you are making a property read-only, you can leave out the getter because it is implied. Now with the setter, you are able to rename one of the fingers of the hand. You rename the pinky to `pinkie`. Now when you print the sentence, it says "I use my pinkie when I drink tea" instead of "I use my pinky when I drink tea." But you don't have to just use integers, and you don't have to return integers, either. You can use this subscript notation however you would like.

Let's take a look at the implementation of a Swift array and how it uses subscripts to access elements of the array. In order to do this, you can type the following into the playground:

```
let a:Array<String> = []
```

This declares an array using the more verbose syntax. You can now hold down the Command key on your keyboard and click the word `Array`. The actual implementation of the array is not included in the source code, but you can see a skeleton of how it was declared. You should see something like this:

```
subscript (subRange: Range<Int>) -> Slice<T>
```

This allows you to access elements of an array by using a range. You can see that the range must be made up of integers. This looks like it's probably only a getter and does not include a setter as well.

You can use subscripts for many things. But you should think about their proper use. For example, you could use a subscript to mess around with a `String`:

```
class Candianizer{
    subscript(sentence:String) -> String {
        return sentence + " ay!"
    }
}
var candianizer = Candianizer()
candianizer["Today is a good day"] //Today is a good day ay!
```

In my opinion, this is not a good use of a subscript. Even though you can use a subscript this way, you generally use them to find elements of a collection, list, or sequence. But you can implement a subscript however you find most appropriate. In the last example you might be better off using a function for `candianizer`.

Dictionaries use subscripts to set and get values for particular instances. You can use subscripts to set a value, like so:

```
var beethovenByOpus = [67:"Symphony No. 5",
    53:"Waldstein",
    21:"Symphony No. 1 in C major"]
beethovenByOpus[67]
```

In this example, you create a dictionary to get some of Beethoven's works, by opus. Now you can access the works by using the subscript syntax. In this example, `beethovenByOpus[67]` prints `"Symphony No. 5"`.

Dictionaries are made up of key/value pairs. In this example, the key is `67`, and the value is `"Symphony No. 5"`. Now the dictionary has the type `Int:String`. You could create a dictionary because you know exactly what you need, but you first need to learn about generics. After you get generics down, you can give it a whirl. For now, you should know that for dictionaries, a subscript is both a getter and a setter. You can make subscripts deal with any input types, and they can use any type for return values as well. However, you cannot use `inout` parameters but you can use multiple parameters to grab any values you want.

Here is an example of creating a multidimensional array for a level of a game. In this example, you use the subscript syntax to grab a specific block from the game:

```swift
class Level {
    //[Array<Int>]
    var map = [[0,0,0,1,1],
               [1,1,1,0,0],
               [1,1,1,0,1]]
    subscript(row:Int,col:Int) -> Int {
        return map[row][col]
    }
}
var level1 = Level()
level1[0,4]
```

It is common to use multidimensional arrays to store game-level data. If you are making a tile-based game, maybe the 0s are walkable ground, and the 1s are non-walkable walls. Say that you want an easy way to grab a specific tile. Normally, if you wanted to grab the first tile in the first row, you would use something like this:

```swift
level1.map[0][0]
```

This works well. But you can make the syntax even nicer by creating a subscript to grab the row and column right from the level:

```swift
level1[0,0]
```

Now you get back the tile straight from the level instead of having to access the map. The really great thing about this is that you could add in error checking to make sure the block exists before you try to access it. Also, this map should be read-only. You could add that at the subscript level, like this:

```swift
struct Level {
    //[Array<Int>]
    var map = [[0,0,0,1,1],
               [1,1,1,0,0],
               [1,1,1,0,1]]
    func rowIsValid(row:Int) -> Bool
        return row < map.count
    }
    func colIsValid(row:Int,col:Int) -> Bool {
        return col < map[row].count
    }
    subscript(row:Int,col:Int) -> Int {
        get{
            assert(rowIsValid(row), "Row does not exist")
            assert(colIsValid(row,col: col), "Column does not exist")
            return map[row][col]
        }
    }
}
var level1 = Level()
```

Check out what happens here: It's super cool. You use Swift's `assert` method to check the validity of the game-level data you are trying to get. You have to send `assert` a `Bool` to say `true` (meaning yes, it is legit) or `false` (meaning no, it is not legit). You make `rowIsValid` and `colIsValid` functions to do that checking for you. The good thing about this is if the user enters a row that is too high or a column that is too high, he or she will get an error message that is geared toward game-level data. Also, the user cannot set the game-level data directly but would have to go through the map, which you could set to be `private`.

That's all you need to know about subscripts for right now. It's all about the way that you want to implement them.

Next we will talk about advanced operators and why it is still important to know how to code on the bit level.

Bits and Bytes with Advanced Operators

Everything you do on computers boils down to bits and bytes, and it's important to be able to understand things on that level. Even though this seems like an old-school idea, it has many real-world and even future implications. For example, if you want to write code to connect to a Bluetooth low-energy device, such as a heart rate monitor, then you need to look at the Bluetooth specifications for such devices (see https://developer.bluetooth.org/gatt/characteristics/Pages/CharacteristicViewer.aspx?u=org.bluetooth.characteristic.heart_rate_measurement.xml). Notice that in order to be able to get the heart rate out of the data from the Bluetooth device, you need to grab specific bytes and bits. This is a current technology and is growing with the presence of iBeacons.

This doesn't apply to just Bluetooth, either; another good example is file specifications. If you ever want to create a binary file specification or read a binary file, then you need to know where different information is going to be in bytes of the file. Take the Photoshop file specification (see http://www.adobe.com/devnet-apps/photoshop/fileformatashtml/). Notice that it tells you exactly where to look in the file and how much data to grab. For example, the header info tells you that the length is 4 and the content should always equal 8BPS. This is an identifier for the file. If you read those first few bits of a Photoshop file, it should say 8BPS. This is similar to when you get a box of animal crackers and it says, "Do not eat if seal is broken." (For me it's always the giraffe that's broken, maybe because of its tall stature and long neck.) Don't assume that it's a Photoshop file unless it has that signature at the beginning.

It's important to note that in Swift, you can represent binary with a `0b` prefix, in the same way that you write hex with a `0x` prefix. Also, a great little trick for binary on a Mac is to open up the built-in calculator. When in the calculator you can then choose View > Programmer to see binary representations of numbers. For example, in decimal, `0b00001111` is 15 (because $1 + 2 + 4 + 8 = 15$; see Figure 7.1).

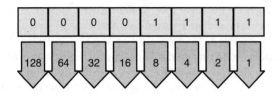

Figure 7.1   Each bit is represented by a square and can have a value of either 0 or 1.

Notice that there are 8 bits here, and all 8 bits together represents 1 byte. For our purposes we are going to read the bits from right to left. Each bit (from right to left) is worth double what the last was worth. To find out what the whole thing is worth, you add the value listed below (values are listed in the arrow below each bit in Figure 7.1) only if the bit (the value in the square) is 1. If the value is 0 you do not add the value of the bit. After you have the value by calculating the 8 bits you can perform different operations on them. Each of these operators is going to do something to the 8 bits of the byte. Some will shift the bytes and others will eliminate bytes. In the end you are left with 8 bits, which represent a byte, which can be trans-lated into letters, numbers, or other stuff (it could be an individual pixel for .png file). Like we said before in the case of the Photoshop file we could be looking for 8BPS to appear in the beginning of the file. Other files types have different signatures. The first advanced operator is bitwise NOT.

Bitwise NOT

You use the bitwise NOT operator when you want to invert all the bits. You write the bitwise NOT as a tilde (~). If you invert 0b00001111, you get 0b11110000, which is 240. You can try this out in playground. You represent the 8 bits as 1 byte by using UInt8. The 8 in UInt8 stands for the number of bits. UInt8 represents 1 byte because it has 8 bits available to store things. This means you have values from 1 to 255 available to you with UInt8. This is the case because if you make all 8 bits set to 1, then 0b11111111 is equal to 255. If you use UInt16, then you have 16 bits available to you, and your max value is much larger, at 65,535. You can try this out in the calculator as we mentioned in the previous section.

Let's get back to inverting bits, which you could do by first assigning your binary value to a variable and then inverting it. Using bitwise NOT takes everything that was a 1 and makes it a 0 and everything that was a 0 and makes it a 1 (see Figure 7.2).

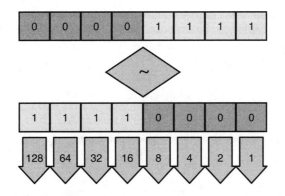

Figure 7.2   Inverting bits with bitwise `not`.

Let's write some code that actually inverts some bits.

```
var b:UInt8 = 0b00001111 // 15
~b // 240
```

In this example we created the number 15 represented in bits. We assigned it to a variable that is of type `UInt8` so we could store those 8 bits in the perfect container for it. You inverted it with the tilde (~) and you got back 240 because `0b00001111` iverted is `0b11110000`. 128 + 64 + 32 + 16 = 240

Bitwise AND

Bitwise `AND` is represented by a single ampersand: `&`. Whereas bitwise `NOT` inverts all the bits, bitwise `AND` changes the bits only if both bits are 1s. For example, say that you have something like what's shown in Figure 7.3.

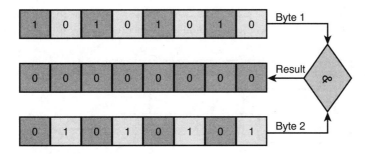

Figure 7.3   Performing a bitwise `AND` on two bytes.

In this example, the result of the bitwise AND combination is 0 because there is no place where both bit 1 and bit 2 contain 1s in the same slot. You could code this example like so:

```
var a:UInt8 = 0b10101010 //170
var b:UInt8 = 0b01010101 //85
a&b //0
```

Figure 7.4 shows another example of a bitwise AND combination that has some *positive* results.

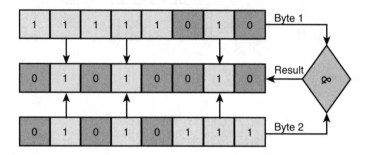

Figure 7.4   Another bitwise AND with more positive results.

In this example, bits of the top byte (all the bits of the first byte) contain 1s where the bits of the bottom byte (bit 2) also does, so the result has some positive results—in spots 2, 4, and 7 from the left. In the playground, you could write this example like so:

```
var a:UInt8 = 0b11111010 //250
var b:UInt8 = 0b01010111 //87
a&b //82
```

Bitwise OR

Bitwise OR is written using a single pipe: |. Whereas bitwise AND returns the new number if both bits are set to 1, bitwise OR returns the new number if either bit is equal to 1 (see Figure 7.5).

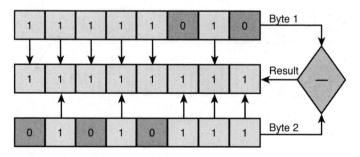

Figure 7.5   Performing a bitwise OR on two bytes with the result in the middle.

When you use the bitwise OR operator, the result is all 1s (255). You can try this out with code like so:

```
var a:UInt8 = 0b11111010 //250
var b:UInt8 = 0b01010111 //87
a|b //255
```

Figure 7.6 shows another example where both inputs are 0, so the resulting bit is 0 also.

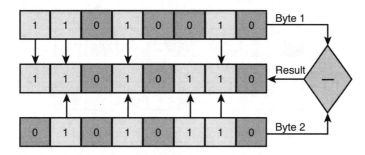

Figure 7.6   Another bitwise OR comparing two bytes.

You could write this comparison as follows:

```
var a:UInt8 = 0b11010010 //210
var b:UInt8 = 0b01010110 //86
a|b //214
```

Bitwise XOR

Otherwise known as the exclusive OR operator, written as ^, bitwise XOR compares two inputs and returns 1 when the two inputs are different (see Figure 7.7).

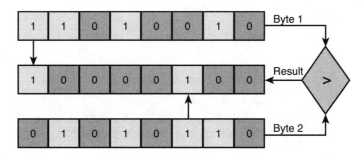

Figure 7.7   Performing a bitwise XOR on two bytes (one on top and one on bottom).

Notice in this example that only the comparisons where input 1 and input 2 are different result in a 1. Matching 1s (1 and 1) returns 0 and matching 0s (0 and 0) returns 0.

Shifting Bits

You can take the 8 bits of a byte and shift them all to the left or to the right. You can do this using the bitwise left shift operator (<<) or the bitwise right shift operator (>>). Notice in Figure 7.8 how each shift is in its own box. You are essentially moving a bit to the next box over.

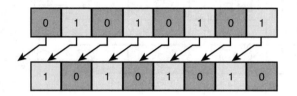

Figure 7.8   Shifting bits to the left.

You could write this in code like so:

```
var a:UInt8 = 0b01010101 //85
a << 1 //170
```

Notice that this bitwise left shift had the effect of doubling the integer. Doing a bitwise right shift, on the other hand, halves the number:

```
var a:UInt8 = 0b01010101 //85
a >> 1 //42
```

Notice that because you are working with integers and not floating-point numbers, you end up with 42 and not 42.5. Also notice that if 1 was the leftmost bit, then this does not necessarily multiply it by 2. This is because the first 1 winds up getting discarded when it moves off the left (see Figure 7.9). Here is an example of the 1 getting discarded:

```
var a:UInt8 = 0b11010101 //213
a << 1 //170
```

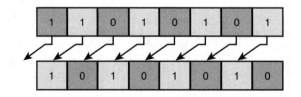

Figure 7.9   Shifting bits.

Any bits that are moved outside the bits of the integer are thrown away. Also note that when a new space is created, as in Figure 7.9, a 0 is inserted. This method is known as *logical shifting*.

UInt8, UInt16, UInt32, Int8, Int16, Int32, and So On

There is a difference between signed and unsigned types. It has nothing to do with autographs. When you have a signed type, it can be positive or negative. The types that start with `Int` are signed and can be either negative or positive. How does Swift represent a negative value in 8 bits internally? The leftmost bit says whether the number is positive or negative. This is how it is represented internally. A 1 as the first bit means the `Int` is negative, and a 0 means positive. Any of the types that are Ints (`Int8`, `Int16`, `Int32`, and so on) use the first bit to say whether the number is negative or positive. If `Int8` has 8 bits available, it now has 7 to represent the number and 1 to represent the sign (see Figure 7.10). UInts (unsigned integers) don't do this. For example, the max value of `UInt8` is 255, and the max value of `Int8` is 127. The leftmost bit was worth 128 so 255–128 and you are left with 127.

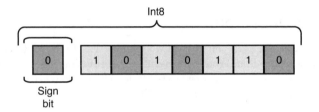

Figure 7.10   A signed byte: the `Int8`.

In code, however, you can represent –4 in binary like so:

```
var a:Int8 = -0b100
```

Value Overflow and Underflow

If you try to fit too much into an `Int` that cannot handle it, you get an error. For example, the max for an `Int32` is 2,147,483,647. You don't have to do math to figure this out. You can figure it out like this:

```
Int32.max // 2,147,483,647
Int32.min // -2,147,483,647
Int16.max // 32,767
// etc...
var a:Int32 = 2_147_483_649 // ERROR: integer literal overflows when stored into 'Int32'
```

In this case, `Int32` is not big enough to hold the number you tried to assign it. It is a little too large (the max is 2147483647 and you tried to use 2147483649), and you get an error. It isn't always desirable or necessary to get an error. You can use value overflow and value underflow to fix this. When you reach the max value of an `Int`, and you add one more, value overflow causes the `Int` to circle back around to the minimum value. Let's watch that `Int` circle back around:

```
var a:Int32 = 2_147_483_647
a &+ 1 // -2,147,483,648
```

This would normally cause an error, but instead it loops around to the minimum value of the `Int`. The opposite happens when you use value underflow. If you are at the minimum of an `Int` and you subtract 1, in order to not get an error, you must use value underflow, like this:

```
var a:UInt8 = 0
a &- 1 // 255
```

This would normally throw an error, but instead it loops back around to the max value of a `UInt8`. We use that ampersand to say we want value underflow and value overflow.

Customizing Operators

Think about the custom `Car` class you've been working with in this book. It has a name, and you could easily add a price to it. What happens if you want to add two cars together? Swift does not know how to do this, so you need to tell it how. You might want to combine cars by name or by price, or you might want to do something else.

You can overload (that is, tell the operators to do something else) all the operators in Swift to do what you would expect for your custom types.

In the case of the custom `Car` class, you have to tell Swift how to add these two things together. Here is a full example of how you can define your own equality operator to see if two "ingredients" are equal:

```
enum DrinkType:UInt8 {
    case Cognac = 1, Bitters, Gin, Dry_Vermouth, Absolut
}
struct Ingredient:Equatable {
    var quantity = 0.0
    var type:DrinkType = .Cognac
}
func == (a:Ingredient,b:Ingredient) -> Bool {
    if a.quantity == b.quantity {
        if a.type == b.type {
            return true
        }
    }
    return false
}
```

```
var someGin = Ingredient(quantity: 2.5, type: .Gin)
var someDryVermouth = Ingredient(quantity: 0.5,type: .Dry_Vermouth)
var someAbsolut = Ingredient(quantity: 2.5, type: .Absolut)

var dryMartini = [someGin,someDryVermouth]
var absolutGibson = [someAbsolut,someDryVermouth]
var availableDrinks = ["Dry Martini":dryMartini,"Absolute Gibson":absolutGibson]

class Drink {
    var contents = [Ingredient]()

    func serveIt() -> String {
        for (key,value) in availableDrinks {
            if contents == value {
                return "Serving \(key)"
            }
        }
        return "Drink not available."
    }
}
var drink = Drink()
drink.contents.append(someGin)
drink.contents.append(someDryVermouth)
drink.serveIt()
```

This is quite a significant example, but I want to make sure you get the gist of why you have to define your own operators. In this example, you define a bunch of ingredients for drinks in an enum. You create an `Ingredient` structure so that you can give a quantity and drink type. Now when you have those quantities and drink types together, you cannot compare them using ==. Try it out. It will not work because you need to first say that the struct itself is `Equatable`. What this really means is that it can be used for comparison with a == operator. Without marking the struct as equatable (you should try this), you get an error when you try to compare two ingredients.

When the `Ingredient` is `Equatable`, you have to define how you are going to compare two ingredients. What you really want here is to make sure the quantity and type are the same. You make a global == function to define what happens when you compare two ingredients. You make it global because that's the way that Swift works. Don't worry: You can define as many of those == functions as you need, as long as you are comparing something other than ingredients. That will make the method signature different—and it will make it legit.

Now you can create a new drink by using the `Drink` class, and you can try to serve the drink. Swift is able to loop through the dictionary of available drinks and compare its current drink contents to see whether it matches a recipe for another type of drink. This example can compare only two ingredients because that is the functionality you wrote. You could also create other operators for this struct as well. Such operators are called *binary operators* because they take two parameters, one on each side of the operator (for example, a == b). You can also create *unary operators*, which operate on only one side (for example, -a or a++). When the operator is on the left, it is called a *prefix unary operator*, and on the right it is a *postfix unary operator*. You could define these for your `Ingredient` class to increase the quantity of the ingredient by 1. Here's how you write that function, which you can add right below your == function:

```
postfix func ++ (inout a:Ingredient) -> Ingredient {
    a.quantity += 1
    return a
}
var someGin = Ingredient(quantity: 2.5, type: .Gin)
someGin++
```

Now you have the ability to create an ingredient and increment its quantity by 1. In this case you are using a postfix operator because you put the operator after the instance of the struct. You use `inout` because you want to modify the object itself. Usually with these unary operators, you use an `inout` parameter. Also note that if you define multiple binary and unary operators, you can use them within each other's definitions. For example, if you defined a binary addition operator, then you could use it to increase the quantity for the definition of the ++ operator.

The only operators you can't redefine are the assignment and ternary operators (that is, a = b and c ? d : e). That one with the question mark is the ternary operator.

Making Your Own Operators

In addition to redefining operators, you can make your own. Custom operators can start with these characters:

```
/ = - + * % < > ! & | ^ . ~
```

They can also start with Unicode math, symbol, arrow, dingbat, and line/box drawing characters. All characters after the first one can be any of the preceding characters and/or Unicode characters. In this section, you'll define the binary ~<*^*>~ operator, just to be extreme. (This arm-flailing-starry-eyed-looking-up operator won't do anything impressive or useful.)

To define an operator, you must use the keyword `operator` and define it as `prefix`, `infix`, or `postfix`, like this:

```
infix operator ~<*^*>~ {}
```

Here you are putting the operator into existence. You haven't actually defined what it does yet.

Next, you define what the operator does. Note that because you use `sqrt` here, you need to import UIKit:

```
func ~<*^*>~ (a:Ingredient,b:Ingredient) -> Ingredient {
    let c = sqrt(a.quantity)
    let d = sqrt(b.quantity)
    let e = pow(c, d)
    return Ingredient(quantity: e, type: a.type)
}
```

```
var someDryVermouth = Ingredient(quantity: 0.5,type: .Dry_Vermouth)
var someAbsolut = Ingredient(quantity: 2.5, type: .Absolut)
var newIng = someDryVermouth ~<*^*>~ someAbsolut
newIng.quantity //0.578115871271409
```

What the operator actually does is up to you. At this point, the new operator is completely useless, but you can see that you can really name your operators however you like.

You have three options when creating operators: infix, prefix, and postfix operators. An infix operator has arguments on both sides of the operator, and the operator you just made is an example of this type. A prefix operator is placed before the argument. Here's an example of this:

```
prefix operator --- {}
prefix func --- (inout a:Ingredient) -> Ingredient {
    a.quantity -= 2
    return a
}
---someGin
```

Here you are creating a triple minus decrement, which will subtract not 1 but 2. It is a prefix operator because you write the triple minus before the variable.

A postfix operator is used after the variable. Here's an example of a custom postfix operator:

```
postfix operator +++ {}
postfix func +++ (inout a:Ingredient) -> Ingredient {
    a.quantity += 2
    return a
}
someGin+++
```

Here you are creating a triple plus increment, which will add not 1 but 2. It is a postfix operator because you write the triple plus before the variable.

Bits and Bytes in Real Life

In this section, you are going to pull in a file and read its bits and bytes. You should be able to decode the file according to the specifications. Let's see what you can do with it. If you are using a Mac, then you already have Python installed, which means you can simply start a local webserver without installing anything. You are going to host a GIF file and read it in. You can use any GIF you want, but I have prepared one for you at http://i.imgur.com/j74SykU.gif.

To start up a new single-view application, follow these steps:

1. Select File > New > Project.

2. Make sure IOS > Application is selected and click on Single View Application.

3. Set Product Name to GIFReader and make sure language is set to Swift.

4. Click Next.

5. On the Save screen, click Create. You now have `AppDelegate.swift`, `Main.storyboard`, and `ViewController.swift`.

6. Open `ViewController.swift` and edit the `viewDidLoad` function, like this:

```
override func viewDidLoad() {
    super.viewDidLoad()
    loadGIF()
}
```

7. Write the skeleton for the `loadGIF` function, like this:

```
func loadGIF() {

}
```

8. Create a new file that does the URL requesting. Call it `Service.swift` and add the following:

```
import UIKit
class Service {
    var url = "http://i.imgur.com/j74SykU.gif"
    func getGIF(callback:(NSData)->()) {
        request(url,callback)
    }
    func request(url:String,callback:(NSData)->()) {
        var nsURL = NSURL(string: url)
        let task = NSURLSession.sharedSession().dataTaskWithURL(nsURL) {
            (data,response,error) in
                callback(data)
        }
        task.resume()
    }
}
```

Here you create a generic request method that requests any data from any URL and returns that data. It is a good amount of code, so you should abstract it away. You use `NSURLSession.sharedSession().dataTaskWithURL(url)` to grab some data from a URL. You could easily modify this to return JSON data as well. If you were writing a larger app, you could write a function like `getPosts`, `getComments`, or `getWhatever`, and all you would have to do is call `request(url,callback)`.

9. Save your file and go back to `ViewController.swift`. Right above the `viewDidLoad` method, as the first line in the class, instantiate your service so you can use it:

```
var service:Service = Service()
```

10. In your new `loadGIF` function, load the GIF:

```
func loadGIF() {
    service.getGIF() {
        (data) in
        println("Got GIF: \(data.length)")
    }
}
```

11. Notice the brevity of the function to load the GIF. You have abstracted away all the messy loading and created a simple closure to load the GIF. You should now have the entire GIF in the `data` parameter, which is of type `NSData`. Now the bits and bytes can begin. Test your app by running it with Command+R. You should see a `trace` statement saying that it got the data and will print out the length. (You can be sure it's the right length if you inspect the real file with Command+I. When I did this, I saw that it was 1.97 MB. The `println` command returned `"Got PSD: 1978548"` for me, which says that the length of the data is in bytes.)

12. Remove `println`. Now you need to take each byte from the data and place each byte into an array. You can use an array of `UInt8`s to divide everything up 1 byte at a time. After these few lines, you will have a new array containing 1 byte per array element. It's not always useful to load everything into memory, but the point of this example is to show you how to work with bits and bytes. You will use the `getBytes` from `NSData`, and you will provide the length of the whole thing. In real life, you might want to load a little bit at a time. Hopefully you aren't using a 300 MB GIF. Change your code like so:

```
func loadGIF() {
    service.getGIF() {
        (data) in
        var bytes = [UInt8](count:data.length, repeatedValue:0)
        data.getBytes(&bytes, length: data.length)
        println(bytes.count)
    }
}
```

Here you create an array of 0 the length of the data. Then you take that array and make a buffer to fill with the data. You basically pass in the `bytes` array like an `inout` parameter, and it fills it up with the right bytes. You can now check the bits and bytes to see whether it conforms to the GIF file specifications. That isn't a whole lot of code, and most of it loads the file.

However, you don't need to store the bytes in an array. Sometimes you will need to do this but not this time. There are even easier ways to read the data. You need to get the first 6 bytes and see if it is equal to `"GIF89a"` or something else. You can do that with one line of code by rewriting `loadGIF()`:

```
func loadGIF() {
    service.getGIF() {
        (data) in
```

```
        println(NSString(data: data.subdataWithRange(NSMakeRange(0, 6)),
    encoding: NSUTF8StringEncoding))
        }
    }
```

Here you use `NSString`, which has an initializer to create a string from data. You don't want all the data; you just want to check the first 6 bytes, so you use `NSMakeRange` to create a range from 0 to 6. You set the encoding to `NSUTF8StringEncoding`. When you run this, the console should say `"GIF89a"` (or something similar). This means the GIF file is legit because version numbers as of July 10, 1990 are `"87a"` for May 1987 and `"89a"` for July 1989.

13. Get the width and height of the file at bytes 7 and 8 and at bytes 9 and 10:

```
func loadGIF() {
    service.getGIF() {
        (data) in
        var current = 0
        var newCurrent = 0
        println(NSString(data: data.subdataWithRange(NSMakeRange(0, 6)),
            encoding: NSUTF8StringEncoding))
        current = 6
        var width = [UInt16](count:1, repeatedValue:0)
        newCurrent = current + 2
        data.getBytes(&width, range: NSMakeRange(current, newCurrent))
        current = newCurrent
        println(width)
        var height = [UInt16](count:1, repeatedValue:0)
        newCurrent = current + 2
        data.getBytes(&height, range: NSMakeRange(current, newCurrent))
        current = newCurrent
        println(height)
    }
}
```

Keep track of where the current byte pointer is. Otherwise, you are going to have to keep a count in your head. You know the width and height come right after the GIF signature. You get the width and height at the next 4 bytes, with 2 bytes each. You use a `UInt16` to represent 2 bytes. Because `UInt8` represents 1 byte, this means a `UInt32` will represent 4 bytes.

14. Now you need to find out whether the gif contains a global color table. And for that you can inspect the first bit of the next byte:

```
var packed = [UInt8](count:1, repeatedValue:0)
data.getBytes(&packed, range: NSMakeRange(current, 1))
var hasGlobalColorTable = false
if packed[0] & 1 == 1 {
    //odd first bit is 1
```

```
        hasGlobalColorTable = true
}
var restOfLogicalScreenDescriptor = 3
current = current + restOfLogicalScreenDescriptor
println(hasGlobalColorTable)
```

15. You grab the next byte by using `UInt8`. You can do a trick to find whether the first bit is a 0 or a 1. By using `& 1`, you can see if that equals 1 and therefore the first bit is 1. You also need to take into account the rest of this block. You add 3 more bytes to account for the rest of logical screen descriptor since you are not using it right now anyway.

As you can see, there are a lot of steps involved in getting all the data out of a GIF file. Here you've seen the gist of reading binary data based on a specification. `UInt8` represents 1 byte, `UInt16` represents 2 bytes, and so on and so forth. Depending on your next size step in the specification, you can grab however large a piece you need (in bytes).

Summary

In this chapter you have learned how to create your own custom syntax. These features are super-duper powerful and can be combined in many different ways. When you combine them with trailing closures and `@autoclosures` (which you will learn about in Chapter 9, "Becoming Flexible with Generics"), the possibilities are endless. You can define your own way of processing data with your own custom operators using your own custom classes made of ASCII pandas and Hebrew letters. You can, technically, use the subscript syntax however you want, but remember that with great power comes great responsibility. You have to be careful not use them as functions but to use them as element assessors.

You've also learned in this chapter that generics give you real power. You can now apply everything from this chapter and the previous ones to create your own dictionaries and custom arrays.

In this chapter, you've also learned how to program at the bit level. In this chapter you've learned how to pull data from a URL and then parse it. You can now take any specification and parse away, and you can also create your own specifications.

8

Protocols

Protocols are at the heart of the iOS architecture; they are first-class paradigms, right up there with classes and structs. They hold a special place because they are the backbone of design patterns such as delegates. Delegates are heavily used in iOS for notifying the programmer when application, UI, and other events happen. You can use a delegate to send a message to everyone who conforms to that protocol. When you use a protocol and all of its offerings, it is called conforming to the protocol.

Protocols themselves don't have any implementation at all—that is, you don't really write code in protocols that does stuff. You can use protocols as a checklist to say, "I need you to write the following methods if you want this thing to work." Protocols describe what must be implemented and what that implementation should look like. You can use protocols with classes, structures, and enumerations. When a class, struct, or enum provides the functionality described in the protocol, you can then say that it is conforming to the protocol.

Writing Your First Protocol

To create a protocol, you start with the keyword `protocol` and then give it a name, followed by a pair of curly brackets. A basic protocol would look like this:

```
protocol MyProtocol {
}
```

You might notice that this newly created protocol is completely empty. Although it is empty, it is valid. The protocol doesn't currently have any functions that it wants you to conform to, but you can provide an implementation of it already. You'll create a class that conforms to `MyProtocol`. It won't be hard to conform to it because it doesn't have any functions to conform to yet. It's like if someone gave me a blank shopping list: I would drive to the supermarket and, when I got there, I would just turn around, because there is nothing to get. Here is the implementation, using a class.

```
class MyClass:MyProtocol {
}
```

The way you tell this class to conform to the protocol is the same way that you tell the class to inherit from another class: You just use the colon followed by the name of the protocol you want implemented. The protocol definition goes inside the curly brackets.

Now you can create an implementation of this protocol. This protocol does not create any requirements, so the class implementation will be just as sparse as the protocol:

```
protocol MyProtocol {

}

class MyClass:MyProtocol {

}
```

If you run this in the playground, you will notice that there are no errors. However, if you add the requirement of a property to the protocol, like this, then the class will need to implement it as well:

```
protocol MyProtocol {
    var someProp:String { get set }
}

class MyClass:MyProtocol {

}
```

Now you'll get an error:

```
:6:1: error: type 'MyClass' does not conform to protocol 'MyProtocol'
class MyClass:MyProtocol {
^
:3:9: note: protocol requires property 'someProp' with type 'String'
var someProp:String { get set }
^
```

What happened? Now you are saying that the protocol has a requirement: A property called someProp must be a getter and a setter. You can fix this error by giving the class the property that the protocol requires. Here's how you do it:

```
protocol MyProtocol {
    var someProp:String { get set }
}

class MyClass:MyProtocol {
    var someProp:String = ""
}
```

When this code runs, the error goes away. You are now strictly adhering to the requirements of the protocol. That is, you are now *conforming* to the protocol.

> **Note**
>
> Notice the words `get` and `set`. In this case, you are saying that `someProp` can be read (that's `get`) and written to (that's `set`).

Properties

This is a good time to talk briefly about getters and setters in Swift. In Swift, you can have a property of a class that is a getter or a setter or both. To see how this works, you'll create a class called `Human`, and then you'll see what it means to get and set properties of that class:

```
class Human {
    var eyeColor = "#00FF00"
    var heightInInches = 68
    var hairLengthInCM = 2.54
    var name = "Skip"
}
```

This class has four properties. You may or may not want all of these properties to be able to be rewritten. For example, once the eye color is set, you might only want that to be able to be read and not written to. There are also other details you can get from these properties being set. For example, you could say that this person's height in a string would be `"medium"`. You can use *computed properties* for this.

The types of variables you have been writing up to this point are called *stored properties*. You can either have a *variable stored property* or a *constant stored property*. You know from Chapter 1, "Getting Your Feet Wet," that you use the keyword `var` to signify a variable stored property and the keyword `let` to signify a constant stored property. You can define a default value of a stored property when you declare it in a class, a struct, or an enum. You did this in the `Human` class with all the properties. You can also change the default value at initialization.

In addition to stored properties, there are, as mentioned earlier, *computed properties*. Computed properties are not stored values; they provide instructions to Swift on how to compute the value of a property. They are used to set and get other stored properties indirectly. You can provide a getter and optionally a setter, as shown here:

```
class Human {
    var eyeColor = "#00FF00"
    var heightInInches = 68
    var hairLengthInCM = 2.54
    var heightDescription:String {
        get {
            if heightInInches >= 92 {
                return "tall"
            } else if heightInInches <= 30 {
                return "short"
            } else {
```

```
                    return "medium"
                }
            }
        }
    }
```

```
var human = Human()
println(human.heightDescription) // medium
```

Here you create a height description, which describes the height of a human, in inches. You are basing this height on the `heightInInches` property of the `Human`. You can create a setter as well if you want to set the height of the person by using a description. Ideally, you would create an enum to describe the different heights available, but for this example you can just use `Strings`, like this:

```
class Human {
    var eyeColor = "#00FF00"
    var heightInInches = 68
    var hairLengthInCM = 2.54
    var heightDescription:String {
        get {
            if heightInInches >= 92 {
                return "tall"
            } else if heightInInches <= 50 {
                return "short"
            } else {
                return "medium"
            }
        }
        set (newHeightDescription) {
            if newHeightDescription == "short" {
                heightInInches = 50
            } else if newHeightDescription == "tall" {
                heightInInches = 92
            } else if newHeightDescription == "medium" {
                heightInInches = 60
            }
        }
    }
}
```

```
var human = Human()
println(human.heightDescription)
human.heightDescription = "short"
println(human.heightInInches)
```

Now you can set the height of the person in inches by using a `String`. You can now use the equal sign on that computed property. You can see this with `heightDescription`, where you use the equal sign to set the height description as a `String`, which in turn sets the height of the human, in inches. Although it isn't the most accurate way of setting a person, it might be helpful in a game where you are creating people on the fly, and you want to create 100 tall people. Instead of hard-coding their heights, you can just set them to be `"tall"`.

In the next example, you set the height from the parameter that was passed in: `newHeightDe-scription`. This is optional as you could rewrite this example and just use the default parameter `newValue`. Here you rewrite just the setter portion of the last example to use a parameter named `newValue` instead of providing a named parameter yourself:

```
set {
    if newValue == "short" {
        heightInInches = 50
    } else if newValue == "tall" {
        heightInInches = 92
    } else if newValue == "medium" {
        heightInInches = 60
    }
}
```

Notice that you don't have to declare a variable here. Instead, you use a variable, called `newValue`, that is available to you in all setters. Many languages with getters and setters use the same variable name `newValue` or `value` or something similar for setters.

Notice that you cannot create read-only stored properties directly. Here's a little trick for creating read-only stored properties: Create a private stored property and a read-only computed property, and you have yourself a read-only stored property. Here is an example of a read-only stored property:

```
class Human {
    private var _name = "Skip"
    var name:String {
        get {
            return _name
        }
    }
}
var human = Human()
println(human.name)
human.name = "Jack"
```

Now you have a property that is being stored, and you have made it read-only. You use the underscore to denote a private variable, but this is only aesthetic so that you can use the variable name `name` twice. This tells the reader that these are the same variable.

The `lazy` Variable

The last topic in our little properties discussion is the `lazy` variable. This variable sits on the couch all day and does absolutely nothing. It's always mooching off you and never cleans his dishes. Actually, `lazy` is pretty handy. You use it to create a variable that is not evaluated until it is actually used. You can declare this variable with the keyword `lazy`. This type of variable is useful when you won't have the initial value of this property until after initialization. Rather than throw an error, you can just tell Swift that you will have the value when you need it, but you just don't have it right now. Here is an example of using the `lazy` keyword, which you don't have at initialization but will have ready when it is needed (it runs once when it's first accessed):

```
class Namer {
    var name:String {
        get {
            //url request for name
            return "Jack"
        }
    }
}


class Human {
    lazy var namer:Namer = Namer()
}
var human = Human() // Namer hasn't been initialized yet.
println(human.namer.name) // Now namer has been initialized
```

In this example, it is possible that the `Namer` class's `name` property won't be ready on initialization. Swift is okay with this, as long as you use the `lazy` keyword to inform Swift that it shouldn't try to grab the value from the `name` class yet.

And now back to your regularly scheduled program on protocols.

`Animizable` and `Humanizable`

In this section, you will make a protocol for the creation of any animal, and call it `Animizable`. This protocol will make sure that anytime someone creates an animal, it will have the proper properties and methods. A lot of times, the names of protocols have `able` at the end. These are some of the Swift standard protocols you will commonly come across:

- **Equatable:** You must overload the `==` operator. This allows you to test your type for equality.

- **Comparable:** You must overload the `<`, `>`, `<=`, and `>=` operators, which will allow you to compare your custom type.

- **Printable:** You must declare a property of type `String` called `description`, which will provide a `String`-based representation of the type.

Methods

You can use a protocol to declare a method requirement. In this case, the adopting implementation must use the methods listed in the protocol in order to conform to it. Here is an example of this situation with your new `Animizable` protocol:

```
enum Food:String {
    case Meat = "meat"
    case Veggies = "veggies"
    case Other = "something else"
}

protocol Animizable {
    var type:String { get }
    func eat(quantityInPounds:Double, what:Food)
}

class Animal:Animizable {
    var type = ""
    func eat(quantityInPounds:Double, what:Food){
        println("I am \(type) and I am eating \(quantityInPounds) pounds of
            \(what.toRaw()).")
    }
}

var human = Animal()
human.type = "human"
human.eat(2,what: .Meat)
```

Here you are creating an `Animizable` protocol, which requires that you add a property type and a method called `eat`. The implementation of the method must have the same parameters as the protocol's definition of the method. If you want `Animizable` to have a type method, then you need to write that in the protocol. You could update the `Animizable` protocol to require a type method called `lbsToKg` as a convenience method to convert pounds to kilograms. You can update your code as follows:

```
protocol Animizable {
    var type:String { get }
    class func lbsToKg(lbs:Double) -> Double
    func eat(quantityInPounds:Double, what:Food)
}

class Animal:Animizable {
    var type = ""
    class func lbsToKg(lbs:Double) -> Double {
        return lbs * 0.453592
    }
    func eat(quantityInPounds:Double, what:Food){
```

```
        println("I am \(type) and I am eating \(quantityInPounds) pounds of
            \(what.toRaw()).")
    }
}
```

Now the protocol requires a type method. You must implement this method when creating your `Animal` class.

This also goes for mutating methods as well: If you want a function to be mutating, you must declare it in the protocol. The implementation of that protocol must then create a mutating method. Mutating is used only for enums and structs. If you implement a protocol that requires a mutating method using a class, then you do not need to write the `mutating` keyword.

Delegation

Delegation is one of the most powerful features of protocols. Delegation is not special to Swift or Objective-C. It is a design pattern, a reusable solution to a common problem within a certain context. A friend of mine described delegation best without even knowing it. He said, "Doesn't a protocol allow you to send messages to anyone who implements that protocol?" Sort of. If you create a new iOS project, the first thing you will most likely see is the `AppDelegate`, which notifies you when certain things happen. For example, in `AppDelegate` there is a method called `applicationWillTerminate`. This method gets called when the application is about to be shut down. It can be called because it adopts `UIApplicationDelegate`. Let's look at how the delegate design pattern works.

Say that you create a protocol called `Humanizable`, where things will happen to `Human` (which adopts `Humanizable`), and you want to notify others of those things:

```
protocol Humanizable {
    var name:String { get set }
    func eat(quantity:Int)
    func play(game:String)
    func sleep()
}
```

You now have a protocol, which can be adopted by any `Human`. You then create a `HumanizableDelegate` protocol that can be adopted in order to be updated with changes to the `Human`. Each function will get an instance of the `Human` that is doing the updating:

```
protocol HumanizableDelegate {
    func didStartEating(human:Humanizable)
    func didFinishEating(human:Humanizable)
    func didStartPlaying(human:Humanizable)
    func didFinishPlaying(human:Humanizable)
    func didStartSleeping(human:Humanizable)
    func didFinishSleeping(human:Humanizable)
}
```

You can now keep track of changes to the Human. You next create a class that conforms to the Humanizable protocol and will have a delegate to do the informing:

```
class Human:Humanizable {
    var name:String
    init(name:String) {
        self.name = name
    }


    var delegate:HumanizableDelegate?

    func eat(quantity:Int) {
        delegate?.didStartEating(self)
        println("Eating \(quantity) pounds of food, yum yum yum")
        delegate?.didFinishEating(self)
    }

    func play(game:String) {
        delegate?.didStartPlaying(self)
        println("I am playing \(game)! So much fun.")
        delegate?.didFinishPlaying(self)
    }

    func sleep() {
        delegate?.didStartSleeping(self)
        println("I am sleeping now. Shhhh.")
        delegate?.didFinishSleeping(self)
    }
}
```

You are now conforming to the Human class. Our Human class implements the actual functionality of the eat, play, and sleep methods of Humanizable. When the instance of the human sleeps we tell our delegate when we have started sleeping and when we have stopped. Now all we have to do is make a human watcher to keep track of all the stuff happening with our human. This class will conform to HumanizableDelegate and truly get informed of changes.

```
class HumanWatcher:HumanizableDelegate {
    func didStartEating(human:Humanizable){
        println("We just were informed that \(human.name) started eating")
    }
    func didFinishEating(human:Humanizable){
        println("We just were informed that \(human.name) finished eating")
    }
    func didStartPlaying(human:Humanizable){
        println("We just were informed that \(human.name) started playing")
    }
    func didFinishPlaying(human:Humanizable){
        println("We just were informed that \(human.name) finished playing")
```

```
    }
    func didStartSleeping(human:Humanizable){
        println("We just were informed that \(human.name) started sleeping")
    }
    func didFinishSleeping(human:Humanizable){
        println("We just were informed that \(human.name) finished sleeping")
    }
}
```

Now you can be completely informed of the Human's activity and do something about it. Even if watching the Human means printing out lines to the console, that's what you'll do. The last thing you need to do is to create the actual instances of the Humans and their Human watchers. The fact that you are using protocols means you can guarantee that the Human will have certain methods. You do not have to worry about those methods not being implemented. Let's create the protocol design pattern using our new human "Jeff":

```
let humanWatcher = HumanWatcher()
let human = Human(name:"Jeff")
human.delegate = humanWatcher
human.play("marbles")
human.sleep()
human.eat(5)
```

```
We just were informed that Jeff started playing
I am playing marbles! So much fun.
We just were informed that Jeff finished playing
We just were informed that Jeff started sleeping
I am sleeping now. Shhhh.
We just were informed that Jeff finished sleeping
We just were informed that Jeff started eating
Eating 5 pounds of food, yum yum yum
We just were informed that Jeff finished eating
```

With the delegate pattern, the delegate of an instance can notify you of things happening in that instance of a class.

Protocols as Types

You know that protocols don't implement any functionality themselves, but that doesn't stop you from using them as parameters or return types in methods. This is where protocols can become extremely powerful. You can use them as a type for a variable or constant, or for arrays and dictionaries.

Here is a protocol that can work for anything that you would like to make walkable:

```
protocol Walkable {
    var name:String { get set }
```

```
        func walk(#numOfSteps:Int)
}
```

Humans can walk and animals can walk, among other actions. Here's how you can make a human that can walk:

```
class Human:Walkable {
    var name = "John"
    func walk(#numOfSteps:Int) {
        println("Human is walking \(numOfSteps) steps")
    }
}
func runWalker(walker:Walkable) {
    walker.walk(numOfSteps:10)
}
var somethingThatWalks = Human()
runWalker(somethingThatWalks)
```

In this example you create a Human class that takes anything that can walk. This works because it adopts the Walkable protocol. You create a top-level function that will walk any Walkable. Notice that the parameter that the runWalker function takes is Walkable. This means anything that adopts the protocol Walkable can be passed in. This gives you a lot of flexibility because now you just call walk on whatever is passed in. You know that what is passed in will have that function available because it adopts Walkable.

Protocols in Collections

Protocols can be used as types, so it shouldn't be a surprise that a protocol can also be used as the type of a collection. Think about the case of the Walkable class from the previous section. Say that you want to create something else that can walk, such as a dog. Here's what you do:

```
class Dog:Walkable {
    var name = "Penny"
    func walk(#numOfSteps:Int) {
        println("The dog is walking \(numOfSteps) steps")
    }
}

let dog = Dog()
let human = Human()
var walkers = [Walkable]()
walkers.append(dog)
walkers.append(human)
for walker in walkers {
    walker.walk(numOfSteps:10)
}
```

Here you have a `Dog` and a `Human`, and they are both `Walkable`. You also have an array that is strictly typed for anything that is `Walkable`. Because the array takes anything that adopts `Walkable`, you can append the `Dog` and the `Human` to the array, and it works just fine. You can imagine that if you took an even more generic protocol, such as `BooleanType`, you could make a very wide-ranging collection.

Protocol Inheritance

You can very easily make protocols inherit other protocols, which will add the requirements on top of one another. To see how this works, in this section, you'll create two other protocols: `Runnable` and `Doggable`. `Runnable` will add one more function requirement: `run()`. `Doggable` will inherit `Walkable` and `Runnable`. `Doggable` will have the requirement of a `bark` function. Because it will implement `Walkable` and `Runnable`, it will also need to implement `walk` and `run` functions. Here's how you create these protocols:

```
protocol Walkable {
    func walk(#numOfSteps:Int)
}

protocol Runnable {
    func run(#howFarInMiles:Float)
}

protocol Doggable: Walkable, Runnable {
    func bark()
}

class Dog: Doggable {
    func walk(#numOfSteps:Int) {
        println("Dog will walk \(numOfSteps) steps")
    }

    func run(#howFarInMiles:Float) {
        println("Dog will run \(howFarInMiles) miles")
    }

    func bark() {
        println("Woof")
    }
}

class FrenchDog:Dog {
    override func bark() {
        println("Le woof")
    }
}
```

```
var dog = Dog()
var leDog = FrenchDog()
dog.bark() // Woof
leDog.bark() // Le woof
```

Here the new `Doggable` class inherits both the `Runnable` and `Walkable` protocols. If you were to not include `walk` or `run` or both in the `Dog` class, Swift would throw an error. The way to have a protocol inherit from other protocols is the same way you use in classes: You create a comma-separated list following the semicolon. You can make a protocol inherit from as many other protocols as you want.

We just talked about how to inherit multiple protocols from other protocols, but how do you adopt multiple protocols at once from a class, a struct, or an enum? We'll look at that next.

Protocol Composition

Protocol composition is a fancy term for making a type adopt multiple protocols at once. If you need to make a type adopt multiple protocols, you use this syntax:

```
protocol<Protocol1, Protocol2>
```

Inside the angled brackets, you place the multiple protocols that you want the type to inherit. When you do this, you are creating a temporary local protocol that has the combined requirements of all the protocols you've listed.

Let's make a sort of powered speaker that uses protocol composition:

```
import UIKit

protocol Powered {
    var on:Bool { get set }
    func turnOn()
    func turnOff()
}
protocol Audible {
    var volume:Float { get set }
    func volumeUp()
    func volumeDown()
}
class Speaker:NSObject, Powered,Audible {
    var on:Bool = false
    var volume:Float = 0.0
    var maxVolume:Float = 10.0

    func description() -> String {
        return "Speaker: volume \(self.volume)"
    }
```

```
func turnOn() {
    if on {
        println("already on")
    }
    on = true
    println("Powered on")
}
func turnOff() {
    if !on {
        println("already off")
    }
    on = false
    volume = 0.0
    println("Powered off")
}
func volumeUp() {
    if volume < maxVolume {
        volume += 0.5
    }
    println("Volume turned up to \(volume)")
}
func volumeDown() {
    if volume > 0 {
        volume -= 0.5
    }
    println("Volume turned down to \(volume)")
}
}
var speakers:[protocol<Powered,Audible>] = []
for n in 1...10 {
    speakers.append(Speaker())
}
func turnUpAllSpeakers() {
    for speaker in speakers {
        turnUpSpeaker(speaker)
    }
}
func turnDownAllSpeakers() {
    for speaker in speakers {
        turnDownSpeaker(speaker)
    }
}
func turnUpSpeaker(speaker:protocol<Powered,Audible>) {
    if !speaker.on {
        speaker.turnOn()
    }
    speaker.volumeUp()
```

```
        println(speaker)
}
func turnDownSpeaker(speaker:protocol<Powered,Audible>) {
        if !speaker.on {
            speaker.turnOn()
        }
        speaker.volumeDown()
        println(speaker)
}
turnUpAllSpeakers()
```

Before I explain anything else, I want to point out some really interesting information. There is a protocol called `Printable`, which allows you to output the textual representation of your type. To adopt `Printable`, you must add a description getter to your class. This does not make your class textual output go out to `println()`. There is also a protocol called `DebugPrintable`, which does the same sort of stuff as `Printable` but it is made strictly for debugging purposes. This protocol also **does not** print to the `println()` output. The only way (as far as I know) to override the output of the `println()` representation of the class is to inherit from `NSObject` and create a description method that returns a `String`. You output the description to that function, and `println()` prints your custom output. Remember, though, that there is no base class in Swift, as there is in JavaScript, Java, and tons of other programming languages. You are not inheriting a description from a grand base class; it just happens to be associated with that class. Also to use `NSObject` make sure you import UIKit or something similar.

The class `Speaker` adopts two protocols: `Powered` and `Audible`. The protocol composition happens in two places. You declare an array that takes only types that adopt those two protocols. You also created a `turnUpSpeaker` method, which takes the temporary protocol, which is made up of the two protocols. Luckily, the `Speaker` class fits the requirements just right, and you can pass in a `Speaker`. You provide `Speaker` with a way to turn on and off and a way to turn the volume up and down. You provide a max volume so you don't exceed that volume, and you check to make sure the speaker is on before you turn it on. You create 10 speakers in a loop, using the `range` operator.

Why would you use protocol composition? Sometimes you have types that must match multiple protocols, and you can create a temporary protocol to meet the requirement.

Protocol Conformity

Sometimes it is necessary to check whether a type is of a protocols type. For example, if you create a `Human` class, which is `Humanizable`, you want to check an array of objects to see whether one of those elements conforms to the protocol. You use the `is` and `as` keywords to downcast the type to check its conformance to the protocol.

Using the keyword `is` returns `true` if the instance conforms to the protocol, and it is a good method to use if you do not need any downcast instance passed along to the inner scope of the `if` statement. If you do need a reference to the downcast instance, you can use the optional `as?` keyword. Here is an example of using both keywords. Notice that there is a little an extra detail you have to add in order to make this possible:

```
import Foundation

@objc protocol Animizable {
    var name:String { get set }
}

@objc protocol Humanizable:Animizable {
    var language:String { get set }
}

@objc protocol Bearable:Animizable {
    func growl()
}

class Human:Humanizable {
    var name:String = "Frank"
    var language:String = "English"
}

class Bear:Bearable {
    var name = "Black Bear"
    func growl() {
        println("Growllll!!!")
    }
}

class Other:Animizable {
    var name = "Other"
}

var lifeCollection:[AnyObject] = [Human(),Bear(),Other()]

for life in lifeCollection {
    println(life)
    if life is Humanizable {
        println("is human")
    }
    if let humanizable = life as? Humanizable {
        println(humanizable.language)
    }
}
```

You have to add the @objc attribute in order to make this work. You use this attribute when you want your Swift code to be available to Objective-C code. However, you are not using it for that purpose here. If you want to check protocol conformance, then you must mark the protocol with that attribute even if you aren't interacting with Objective-C code.

You can see that when you use the `as?` optional, you are able to call the `language` attribute of the `Human`, which would otherwise be just `AnyObject`. If you tried to get the `language` property of the `Human` from the `is` downcast, you would get an error: `error: 'AnyObject'` `does not have a member named 'language'`. This is because you never actually downcast the `AnyObject` to a `Humanizable`. This is very powerful because you have protocols that inherit other protocols. You would get a wider range if you checked for the conformance of `Animizable`.

> ### Note
> The `@objc` attribute can be adopted only by classes, and not by structures or enums.

When you are looping through the array, you check for the conformance of the protocol with both `is` and `as?`. In the case of `as?`, if there is a match and the element does conform to the protocol, the optional is unwrapped and assigned to the `let`, using optional binding. At that point, the element of the array is no longer `AnyObject` but is known as type `Humanizable`. The object itself is not changed but merely temporarily downcast when it is stored in the constant.

Optional Protocol Prerequisites

If you peruse the Swift pseudo-code by Command+clicking protocols, you will see that a lot of them have optional requirements. For example, when you start a new project of any type, you can inspect `UIApplicationDelegate`, and you should see something like what Figure 8.1 shows.

```
protocol UIApplicationDelegate : NSObjectProtocol {

    optional func applicationDidFinishLaunching(applicatio
    @availability(iOS, introduced=6.0)
    optional func application(application: UIApplication,
        AnyObject]?) -> Bool
    @availability(iOS, introduced=3.0)
    optional func application(application: UIApplication,
        AnyObject]?) -> Bool

    optional func applicationDidBecomeActive(application:
    optional func applicationWillResignActive(application:
    optional func application(application: UIApplication,
        point, please replace with application:openURL:sou
    @availability(iOS, introduced=4.2)
    optional func application(application: UIApplication,
        AnyObject?) -> Bool // no equiv. notification. ret

    optional func applicationDidReceiveMemoryWarning(appli
        possible. next step is to terminate app
    optional func applicationWillTerminate(application: UI
    optional func applicationSignificantTimeChange(applica
        savings time change

    optional func application(application: UIApplication,
        UIInterfaceOrientation, duration: NSTimeInterval)
    optional func application(application: UIApplication,
        UIInterfaceOrientation)

    optional func application(application: UIApplication,
        coordinates
    optional func application(application: UIApplication,
```

Figure 8.1   The `UIApplicationDelegate` protocol.

You can see that most of the methods of this protocol are optional and therefore do not need to be implemented. You can mark any method as optional so that the compiler will not throw an error if a method is not implemented. Even though you can't see it in Figure 8.1, you need to mark a protocol with the @objc attribute if you plan on creating an optional method. This is true even if you are not planning on making your code available to Objective-C.

Let's look at a quick example. Apparently, bears cough when they are scared. So in this example, you create an optional cough method of the Bearable protocol:

```
import Foundation

@objc protocol Animizable {
    var name:String { get set }
}

@objc protocol Humanizable:Animizable {
    var language:String { get set }
}

@objc protocol Bearable:Animizable {
    func growl()
    optional func cough() //Apparently bears cough when they are scared.
}

class Human:Humanizable {
    var name:String = "Frank"
    var language:String = "English"
}

class Bear:Bearable {
    var name = "Black Bear"
    func growl() {
        println("Growllll!!!")
    }
    //Bear does not implement the cough method. He never gets scared.
}
```

Notice that you do not implement the cough method for the Bear class. You do not need to implement it because the protocol is marked optional for that method.

There is a possibility that you will try to call a method that does not exist at this point because it may not be implemented. In this case you would use optional chaining, discussed next.

Optional Chaining

When you have optional methods that may or may not exist, you need to be able to call them without the possibility of crashing your program. Did you think that the optional methods in protocols are just optional, meaning that you can include them or not include them? If you did, you were wrong. They are directly tied to optionals and can be checked via value binding.

Using optional chaining is another possibility instead of forcing the unwrapping of optionals. The big difference between optional chaining and forced unwrapping is that whereas forced unwrapping gives you an error and crashes your program if the thing you are looking for does not exist, optional chaining does not.

When you have an optional method that may or may not exist, you can use optional chaining to test for the existence of the method. To see how this works, you can expand your `Bear` example, like this:

```
class Bear {
    var name = "Black Bear"
    var paws:Paws?
    func growl() {
        println("Growllll!!!")
    }
    //Bear does not implement the cough method. He never gets scared.
}
class Paws {
    var count = 4
}
var bear:Bear = Bear()
bear.paws = Paws()
println(bear.paws?.count) // Optional(4)
```

What is super interesting about this example is that the count of the paws returns an optional when it clearly was not set as an optional. That's what optional chaining does for you: It allows you to safely write code with optionals in the middle. Let me explain a little further. The bear has optional paws. (Obviously, in a real-life bear, paws are never optional, but in this situation, they might be optional.) When you create a new `Bear`, you do not know whether the paws will exist or not. So you mark the paws as optional, like this:

```
bear.paws?
```

Now this is going to return either an instance of the paws as an optional or `nil`. The program cannot crash at this point because you will either get optional paws or `nil`. Optional chaining then marks everything within the optional paws as optional as well, even if it weren't optional. So the `count` within the paws will become an optional `Int`. This is because the paws may not exist, so everything within the paws may not exist as well, and you don't want the program to crash because of that. When you grab the `count`, like this, it is now an optional or `nil`, depending on whether the paws exist:

```
bear.paws?.count
```

This returns an optional, so now you can perform optional binding to get the unwrapped optional out:

```
if let count = bear.paws?.count {
    println("The count was \(count)")
} else {
    println("There were no paws")
}
```

Now you can test for the existence of the paws and get the `count` out of the optional that it was placed in.

> **Note**
>
> The biggest takeaway here is this: The paws may or may not have existed, and therefore everything within the paws had to be made an optional in order to not crash the program. That is the technique is called *optional chaining*. If one link of the chain is broken, then the whole thing crashes.

Back to Optional Protocol Requisites

With optional chaining tools in hand, you can now test to see whether your methods exist:

```
@objc protocol Bearable {
    func growl()
    optional func cough() -> String //Apparently bears cough when they are scared.
}

@objc class Bear:Bearable {
    var name = "Black Bear"
    func growl() {
        println("Growllll!!!")
    }
}

@objc class Forest {
    var bear:Bearable?
    func scareBears() {
        if let cough = bear?.cough?() {
            println(cough)
        } else {
            println("bear was scared")
        }
    }
}
var forest = Forest()
forest.scareBears()
```

You check whether the `Bearable` implementation exists with optional chaining. You assign the return of the method with optional binding, and if it is not `nil`, you print the output of the method; otherwise, you just print `"the bear was scared"`.

Multiple chaining is going on in this situation. First, you check the optional `bear`, which could be `nil`. Then you check the optional `cough` method, which could also be `nil` and not implemented.

Useful Built-in Swift Protocols

Swift has a solid group of protocols you can implement in your classes to make stuff happen. The following sections describe them.

The `Equatable` Protocol

You use `Equatable` when you want one class to be comparable to another class, using the `==` operator. For example, if you have two `Car` classes that you want to compare for equality, you could adopt the `Equatable` protocol. You have to implement the `==` function (which can only be written on a global level), as shown here:

```
class Bear:Equatable {
    var name = "Black Bear"
    func growl() {
        println("Growllll!!!")
    }
}
func == (lhs:Bear, rhs:Bear) -> Bool {
    return lhs.name == rhs.name
}
var bear1 = Bear()
bear1.name = "Black Bear"
var bear2 = Bear()
bear2.name = "Black Bear"
println(bear1 == bear2) //true
```

Here you are comparing two bears. You would not normally be able to do this because Swift would not know how to compare two bears. Thankfully, you can let Swift know how to compare them. In this case, you have Swift compare the bears by name. If the names are the same, then the bears are considered equal.

The `Comparable` Protocol

The `Comparable` protocol allows you to compare two objects by using at least the `<` operator. You can also override the other operators: `>`, `>=`, and `<=`. Consider that the less-than operator is required by law and Apple, and must be implemented on the global scope. Here's how you can update the `Bear` class to make bears comparable by weight:

```
class Bear:Equatable,Comparable {
    var name = "Black Bear"
    var weight = 0
    func growl() {
        println("Growllll!!!")
    }
}

func == (lhs:Bear, rhs:Bear) -> Bool {
    return lhs.name == rhs.name
}

func < (lhs:Bear, rhs:Bear) -> Bool {
    return lhs.weight < rhs.weight
}

var bear1 = Bear()
bear1.name = "Black Bear"
bear1.weight = 275
var bear2 = Bear()
bear2.name = "Black Bear"
bear2.weight = 220

println(bear1 == bear2)
println(bear1 < bear2) // false
```

Here you are implementing the Comparable protocol to give Swift a way to compare the bears by using at least the less-than operator. You then write the global less-than function and give it two parameters of type Bear. You can make as many of those global functions as you need, as long as the parameters that it accepts are different.

The Printable Protocol

The Printable protocol allows you to provide a textual representation of a class, a struct, or an enum. It is supposed to be able to be used by println, but that does not work as you would expect. It does make your life a whole lot simpler when creating text, though. Instead of having to write something like "my bear is \(bear1.name)", you can just write "my bear is \(bear1)". Printable works in an app but not in the playground or in the REPL (the command line Swift compiler, which can be run in Terminal using xcrun swift). You can add this protocol to be adopted by the Bear class like so:

```
class Bear:Equatable,Comparable,Printable {
    var name = "Black Bear"
    var weight = 0
    var description:String {
        return self.name
    }
```

```
    func growl() {
        println("Growllll!!!")
    }
}

func == (lhs:Bear, rhs:Bear) -> Bool {
    return lhs.name == rhs.name
}

func < (lhs:Bear, rhs:Bear) -> Bool {
    return lhs.weight < rhs.weight
}

var bear1 = Bear()
bear1.name = "Black Bear"
bear1.weight = 275
println("Our bear is \(bear1)")
var bear2 = Bear()
bear2.name = "Black Bear"
bear2.weight = 220
println("Our bear is \(bear2)")

println(bear1 == bear2)
println(bear1 < bear2)
```

Again, `Printable` does not work in playground or the Swift REPL. If you want to print to `println` in the playground or the REPL, a trick is to inherit from `NSObject` to create a function description that returns a `String`. You also have to delete `Printable` and its description from the computed property. Here's what this trick looks like:

```
class Bear:NSObject, Equatable,Comparable {
    var name = "Black Bear"
    var weight = 0
    func description() -> String {
        return self.name
    }
...
```

I am not sure if this is a bug in Swift or intended, but either way, this is a decent workaround.

The `DebugPrintable` Protocol

`DebugPrintable` is the same as `Printable` but used for debugging purposes. For its implementation, you use `debugDescription` instead of `description`. This protocol also does not work in the playground or the Swift REPL.

Summary

In this chapter you have learned how to create protocols of many different varieties. You've learned how to check for optional protocol methods and properties. There are many more protocols available to you in the Swift library. The ones described in this chapter are the most important ones to remember and will come in handy.

This chapter describes how to create a protocol and all the different ins and outs of protocols, but in the end, it is up to you to know the right time for a protocol. After practicing with them for a while, I began to find myself using them more often and in really neat ways. For example, I created a text-based game in which anything that was able to be picked up fell into a protocol I created called `PickableUpable`. I then passed around `PickableUpables` instead of looping through each different thing that could be picked up. Then, using optional downcasting, I checked whether each item was the `PickableUpable` that I wanted. Sure, I could have called it `PickUpable`, but what fun would that be?

When you combine protocols with generics, you'll have a lot of power. You already have some great tools for abstracting code and making it reusable. With generics you will be able to apply your protocols to generics to make methods work with any type of object that meets certain criteria.

9

Becoming Flexible
with Generics

Generics are an awesome feature of Swift that allow you to accept more generic types when creating methods, parameters, properties of classes, and so on. Generics allow you to abstract away functionality that would have been repetitious to write. Sometimes you want to write a function that takes not just Ints, *but* Ints *as well as* Strings *and anything* Printable. *Without generics, you would have had to write a method multiple times for each type. With generics, you can now write one method for all acceptable types. They're called generics because you are creating generic versions of a method. The exact type that you accept has not been decided yet. When you write generics, you are removing duplication while showing your intentions. When you examine the Swift pseudo-source code, you'll notice (when you read this chapter) that a good deal of Swift is written using generics. Take, for example, arrays, which can act as collections for* **any** *type. You can put* Strings, Ints, *or any other type inside an array. The same goes for dictionaries and many other things in Swift. By using generics, they didn't have to write an array for* String, *then an array for* Ints, *and so on. They wrote one array implementation and told Swift to accept a generic type. You might take it for granted that you can use any type with an array, but you should know that it possible because of generics.*

The Problem That Generics Solve

Let's talk about the problem that generics solve. Consider this function, which swaps two integers:

```
func swapTwoInts(inout a: Int, inout b: Int) {
    let temporaryA = a
    a = b
    b = temporaryA
}
var a = 10
var b = 1
```

```
swapTwoInts(&a,&b)
println(a) // 1
println(b) // 10
```

This works just as expected. You are able to swap the two Ints by passing them as inout parameters to the function. The *problem* is that this function only works with Ints. If you try setting the variables to 10.5 (a double) or "Hello there" (a string), it will not work because 10.5 is a Double and "Hello there" is a String. This function only takes Ints. The function's implementation itself (the code inside the function) is generic enough to take any of the other types, but the problem is the parameter's type. If you want to use this function for Doubles and Strings, you have to rewrite it for Doubles and then again for Strings. If you do that, you get a lot of repetition.

This is where generics come in. By creating a generic form of the function, you allow the function to accept any type. This will fix the problem of repeating yourself. Generics add even more power because you can limit the types it accepts by using protocols. That way you won't get errors when you're trying to run a function with parameters it isn't meant for. For example, you may use a generic that only accepts types that adopt Equatable, then anything that is not Equatable will not be allowed. It's better to throw errors before the user compiles the code rather than crashing the program. Here's how you could reimplement your swap to use generics:

```
func swapValues<T>(inout a:T, inout b:T) {
    let temporaryA = a
    a = b
    b = temporaryA
}

var a = "hi"
var b = "bye"

swapValues(&a, &b)
println(a) // "bye"
println(b) // "hi"
```

This function looks almost exactly the same as the previous one. The difference is that special T in brackets. You haven't seen this yet. After adding the T you can use this function with Strings. You could also now use this function with Ints, or Doubles, or any other data type. The T declares a type. However, this code does not describe what that type is. T is a placeholder for the type that will be sent via the parameters. That placeholder is used to act as the same type for your parameters. What type T is will be determined when the function is run. It all depends on what type you send the function.

By putting that T in angle brackets, you are saying to Swift "Do not look for a specific type now, I will tell you the type once the function is run." Then, as long as both parameters are the same type (because you used T for both; if you had used T and U or something else, T and U will represent different types), the function will work. Even though the T is not any specific type. This means that you can't pass two different types, like an Int and a String; you must pass the same type. The angle brackets at the beginning of the function tell Swift it is dealing with a generic type.

> **Note**
>
> You don't have to use T here, though; you can use anything you want. And, in fact, you can use multiple names. It is customary to use a single capital letter for generic types but, you can do whatever you want. It is also customary to use capital camel case when naming generic types. Using the same letter represents the same type, meaning that whatever type you decide to send in must match other types with the same name.

Other Uses for Generics

In addition to creating functions with generic types, you can also provide your own custom types, using classes, structs, and enums. The array type is a good example of this. Notice that when you create an array, you are setting the type at creation time:

```
var a:[Int] = [1,2,3]
```

Notice that the preceding example tells the array to use Ints. Here's another way to do this:

```
var a:Array<Int> = [1,2,3]
```

This syntax is the generic syntax for an array. It tells you that what appears after the equals sign is an array made of Ints. Inside those angled brackets you declare that the array uses Ints. An array is just a list or sequence. You can create your own array-like structure that has a similar implementation to the array but with your own added functionality. Let's call this custom array-like structure a List, and this List will use a method named add instead of append.

Here's how you can make a List type that accepts and works with any type:

```
class List<T> {
    var items = [T]();
    func add(item:T){
        items.append(item)
    }
    var count:Int {
        return items.count
    }
    subscript(i: Int) -> T {
        return items[i]
    }
}

var l = List<Int>()
l.add(1)
l.add(2)
```

```
l.add(3)
println(l.count)
```

In this new `List` class, when you set the type during initialization, you can also add `Int`s to `List`. This `List` is a generic type, which means it is a type that can work with multiple *types*. It will work with those types in the same way that arrays and dictionaries work with any type. When you define `T` as `<T>`, you are declaring that this *generic* type will be used throughout the rest of your code and represent one type. When using the generic type, if you were to instantiate `T` as an `Int`, then anywhere you used `T` in the class, it will be considered an `Int`.

Within the code, you create an array of `T`s (whatever `T` will be, once the class is instantiated). You allow the user to access the array of `T`s through the use of a subscript. This means you can get items from the list like so:

```
println(l[2])
```

Now you have created your own array-like structure. Notice that if you try to loop through the list, you will get an error. That is because you didn't implement iterating for your custom type. The point is that you have a custom type called `List`, which has its own `append`-like method but does not have any of the other array methods. It is a light array, or diet array. Whatever type you assign when creating the `List` is the type that the `List` will use. `List` uses `T` as a generic type that will be defined at the time of creation. Also note that `T` could be a struct, an enum, a class, or a protocol—as long as it falls under the category of type.

Let's improve the list to make it more useful:

```
class List<T:Equatable> {
    var items = [T]();
    func add(allItems:T...){
        items += allItems
    }

    func deDup() {
        var uniques = [T]()
        for t in items {
            if find(uniques,t) == nil {
                uniques.append(t)
            }
        }
        items = uniques
    }

    func indexOf(item:T) -> Int {
        for (index,t) in enumerate(items) {
            if t == item {
                return index
            }
        }
    }
```

```
        return -1
    }

    var count:Int {
        return items.count
    }
    subscript(i: Int) -> T {
        return items[i]
    }
}

var l = List<Int>()
l.add(1,2,3,4,5,4,4,4,5,6,7,7)
l.deDup()
println(l.indexOf(10))
println(l.count)
```

There are a bunch of changes in this version of List. First, you declare the type of this List as T:Equatable. This means that any type you use must adopt the protocol Equatable. You need to use only types that implement Equatable in order to implement a JavaScript-style indexOf function because it needs to match types. In order to find a match you need to use a ==. Only types adopting Equatable can use ==.

Swift has a bunch of global functions that come packaged and ready to use. One of them is the find function. find takes an array and that thing you are searching for as parameters. It returns an optional Int, and nil if it can't find that thing you are looking for. This is the proper way of searching an array in Swift. However, I've always liked JavaScript's indexOf function, which returns -1 if it can't find what you are looking for and returns the index of your found item if it finds a match.

You implemented indexOf by using Swift's enumerate function to loop through an array while also grabbing the index. The code will compare the item you are looking for with the current item in the array. If it cannot find that item, it returns -1. If a match is found, it returns the index at which it was found. This is possible only because you can compare the equality of two objects. In order for this to work, those two objects must be Equatable. That is why this List must use a generic type that is Equatable. This concludes the implementation of your JavaScript-like indexOf function. Nice job!

You have also created a deDup function, which removes all duplicates of the array, also using Swift's find function. deDup works by creating a new array and pushing all the unique items into that array by first checking whether they exist, using Swift's find function.

You also added some new functionality to the add method. The add method now takes any number of arguments and adds them into the list—overall a major improvement.

Generics for Protocols

Protocols can create/define generic types called *associated types*. You may sometimes want
to create a protocol that uses some type that will be decided when you create the object.
Earlier in the chapter, you created a `List` that has a couple of nifty methods and properties.
Now you will create a protocol to describe some of the functionality. So here you'll create a
`Bucket` protocol to describe the adding functionality to the `List`, so that you can add as many
elements as you want—and remove them. You'll also make a `Uniquable` protocol, which
describes the `deDup` functionality. Here are the two protocols and their implementation declaration in the `List`:

```
protocol Bucket {
    typealias SomeItem
    var count:Int { get }
    func add(allItems:SomeItem...)
    func indexOf(item:SomeItem) -> Int
    subscript(i:Int) -> SomeItem { get }
}


protocol Uniquable {
    func deDup()
}


class List<T:Equatable>:Bucket, Uniquable {
```

`List` is now fitted with two protocols it claims to adopt: `Bucket` and `Uniquable`. For the
`Bucket` protocol, notice that you declare a `typealias` for `SomeItem`. You don't know the
type of `SomeItem` right now, but when the `List` gets created, `SomeItem` will be the same type
as `T`. You declare the `add` method to take a type of `SomeItem`. You also declare `indexOf` to
take a type of `SomeItem`. Notice that you do not need to declare `SomeItem` for the `Uniquable`
protocol because the `deDup` functionality does not need it in its method signature in order to
operate. The `List` class already implements both of these protocols. When creating protocols,
you can use that `typealias` of `SomeItem` (and you can name it whatever you want) anywhere
you would need to declare the generic type that is used in the class, struct, or enum in which
you are declaring the generic type.

In order to conform to the `Bucket` protocol, you need to implement the following:

- A property count

- An `add` method that takes a variadic parameter named `allItems` of type `SomeItem` so
  that you can add as many items as you like

- An `indexOf` method that takes a parameter named `item` of type `SomeItem` and returns
  an `Int` (This way you can see, using `indexOf`, whether a specific item exists in the `List`.)

- A subscript so you can directly access the members of the `List` and that returns a type of
  `SomeItem`

In order to conform to the `Uniquable` protocol, you need to implement only one method, `deDup`, which takes no parameters and returns nothing. Because this method does not use the generic type in its signature, you do not need to declare the `typealias` of `SomeItem` for it.

The `List` class already provides an implementation for these requirements, so you are good to go there as well.

The `where` Clause

If you wanted to provide an extra utility knife for the `List` collection, you could write a couple functions that do some useful stuff to the `List`. You will have very strict criteria for the parameters of the function, even more strict than a protocol. Enter the `where` clause! You can specify that parameters must meet certain criteria before being passed in. This of it like a bouncer at a club. Let's say you were comparing two `Lists`—you would want to make sure that both `Lists` being passed in meet the criteria of a `List`. You could make a function that will combine all `Lists` passed in and `deDup` them all at once, leaving you with one list with all unique values:

```
protocol Bucket {
    typealias SomeItem
    var count:Int { get }
    var items:[SomeItem] { get set }
    func add(allItems:SomeItem...)
    func add(allItems:[SomeItem])
    func indexOf(item:SomeItem) -> Int
    subscript(i:Int) -> SomeItem { get }
}
```

There is a functionality that Swift arrays currently do not have but I really wish they did. The functionality—passing an array to a variadic parameter—is otherwise known as the splat operator in other languages. You can implement this functionality yourself. The implementation looks like this:

```
class List<T:Equatable>:Bucket, Uniquable {
    var items = [T]();
    func add(allItems:T...){
        items += allItems
    }
    func add(allItems:[T]) {
        items += allItems
    }
...
```

Now you are ready to create the new `combineUnique` function. This function will combine two arrays and then remove the duplicates. It is important to carefully watch what *types* are passed into this function. That is why you need to implement the `where` clause here. Here's what you need:

```
func combineUnique<L1:Bucket,L2:Bucket
    where L1.SomeItem == L2.SomeItem, L1:Uniquable>(list1:L1,list2:L2) -> L1 {
    list1.add(list2.items)
    list1.deDup()
    return list1
}
```

Take a look at this super-meaty `where` clause. Here's what's going on:

- First are the angle brackets with the two generic types declared:

  `<L1:Bucket, L2:Bucket`

  This says that you will use two different generic types in this function, and both must adopt the `Bucket` protocol.

- The `where` clause compares the `typealias` of `L1` and `L2`:

  `where L1.SomeItem == L2.SomeItem`

  This means that the items in `L1` and `L2` must be the same. They can be whatever you want, but they must be of the same type. They can both be `Ints`, or both be `Strings`, or whatever you want, as long as they are the same type.

- A comma says that one more condition must be met. You want to make sure that `L1` adopts the protocol `Uniquable`:

  `L1:Uniquable`

  You need to do this because you will need to `deDup` the first list after you add `list2`'s items to it.

So, the `where` clause must meet the following criteria: The types of `list1` and `list2` must adopt the `Bucket` protocol, *and* the items contained within `list1` and `list2` must be of the same type, *and* `list1` must adopt the protocol `Uniquable`.

Providing such a strict `where` clause means that the actual code (the implementation) that makes this happen is very short. You abstracted away some of the dirty work and gave it to the implementation of the `Bucket` protocol. You don't need to write the code that combines arrays or the code that removes the duplicates. All you need to do is write the two lines of code that do the removal of duplicate elements, and you are done. You know that this method will work because of the strict `where` clause. You gave this method strict guidelines to abide by and by doing so the developer who uses this code will be greeted with errors before he compiles the code. Classes must meet certain criteria to even be considered for this function.

You might be wondering, as I did, why you need all these complicated `where` clauses in a function. Why can't you just use one type: `L1:Bucket, Uniquable`? Because you need to combine the lists, and in order to do that, the contents of the lists must be the same type. You can't combine a list of `Ints` and `Strings`, because that would not work. You need to make sure the junk in `list1` is the same type as the junk in `list2`. If you left it as `L1:Bucket, Uniquable`, then you could make two different lists with different types and pass them in.

This way of using `where` clauses also frees you up to spend time doing error checking. You know that anything that got into this function meets the requirements of this function. You don't need to do any downcasting or type checking because the `where` clause does that for you.

Now it would be really nice if you could see the contents of this array that you've deDuped and combined. In order to do that, you need to implement a generator so that it can loop through the contents of the array. You could implement your own generator, but you can also take a shortcut to implement it. Because the items of your `List` form an array, and arrays have the implementation of looping already built in, you can use an array, like this:

```
protocol Bucket {
    typealias SomeItem
    var count:Int { get }
    var items:[SomeItem] { get set }
    func add(allItems:SomeItem...)
    func add(allItems:[SomeItem])
    func indexOf(item:SomeItem) -> Int
    subscript(i:Int) -> SomeItem { get }
}


protocol Uniquable {
    func deDup()
}


class List<T:Equatable>:Bucket, Uniquable, SequenceType {
    var items = [T]();
    func add(allItems:T...){
        items += allItems
    }

    func add(allItems:[T]) {
        items += allItems
    }

    func deDup() {
        var uniques = [T]()
        for t in items {
            if find(uniques,t) == nil {
                uniques.append(t)
            }
        }
        items = uniques
    }

    func generate() -> IndexingGenerator<Array<T>> {
        return items.generate()
    }
}
```

```
    func indexOf(item:T) -> Int {
        for (index,t) in enumerate(items) {
            if t == item {
                return index
            }
        }
        return -1
    }

    var count:Int {
        return items.count
    }
    subscript(i: Int) -> T {
        return items[i]
    }
}

func combineUnique<L1:Bucket,L2:Bucket
    where L1.SomeItem == L2.SomeItem, L1:Uniquable>(list1:L1,list2:L2) -> L1 {
    list1.add(list2.items)
    list1.deDup()
    return list1
}

var l = List<Int>()
l.add(1,2,3,4,5,4,4,4,5,6,7,7)
var l2 = List<Int>()
l2.add(1,2,3,4,5,4,4,4,5,6,7,7,8,9,10)
println(combineUnique(l,l2).count)
for n in l {
    println(n) // 1,2,3,4,5,6,7,8,9,10
}
```

The main idea behind making your class loopable is to make your class/struct adopt the SequenceType protocol. The SequenceType protocol wants you to create a function called generate that returns some sort of generator. You could write one yourself by subclassing one of the many generators. Instead, here you took a shortcut and used the items generator that is already built into the array. Of course, you could always start with a blank slate and implement the whole thing, but you didn't need to.

Summary

Generics provide a great way to abstract your code so that when you create a new fancy List type, it will work the same for a list of Strings, Ints, or even NSDates. Generics give you a great way to write code that is type safe so that instead of writing code to check types, you can rest assured that types are coming in as you expect them to.

10

Games with SpriteKit

In Chapter 5, "Making a Game," you created a tic-tac-toe game with basic graphics. As you did so, you also learned how to organize code for a game by using things like classes, functions, and structs. While this chapter continues to build on those concepts, it focuses more on animation. For tic-tac-toe, you wrote code to change the X and O graphics each time a player touched the game board. This worked well for that small project, but would it work for games that involve frame-based animation? For such games, you should consider using Apple's SpriteKit library. SpriteKit gives you an infrastructure for handling many aspects of game creation. This chapter focuses on how it helps with 2D animation, basic physics, and sound playback.

In this chapter, you will make a platform game as an example. The hero, a spinning ball, will roll along an animated platform. Barriers will spawn on the path, requiring the hero to leap over them. A text area will display the score, and a basic start screen with a play button will draw users into the action. When you're finished building the game, it should look as shown in Figure 10.1.

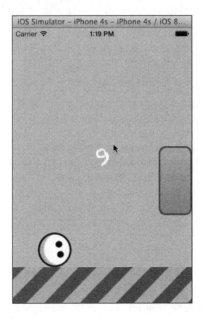

Figure 10.1   The game in action.

Setting Up the Project

To create a new project in Xcode 6, navigate to File > Project in the top menu. For this game, you need to configure only a few settings. Start by selecting Game for the application type. You can make up your own title but make sure that the target device is set to Universal. Once you click Create, Xcode leads you into the new project and presents some options for further configuration. Under the Deployment Info tab, only Portrait should be checked. Click the play symbol in the upper-left corner of Xcode to preview the app. If you set up the project correctly, you should see the screen shown in Figure 10.2.

Figure 10.2   The default SpriteKit game.

Xcode presents a simple default game. It illustrates the use of frames and nodes, two topics that we'll soon discuss in greater detail. Now that you've created a project, take a moment to familiarize yourself with the Xcode layout. The left-hand panel lists game resources such as classes and image assets. Click Main.storyboard to reveal the game's main user interface, where most of the action takes place. You may notice that Main.storyboard has an irregular shape. It doesn't look like an iPhone or an iPad. That's because the game's layout can adapt automatically to both devices.

With Main.storyboard open, take a look at the panel wedged between our main user interface and the list of resources. You should see a group of items under the heading Game View Scene Controller. Click an item, such as View, and select the Inspect Properties icon in the right-hand panel. Notice that you can assign a custom class to the view. By default, all view classes in the game inherit from SKView. This is a base class from which all views extend. In the future, you might want views to inherit properties from other classes. For now, you should keep it simple and stick to one controller that inherits from SKView.

Loading a Scene View

Navigate to the GameViewController class. If you created the program in Chapter 5, viewDid-Load may appear familiar. This method is called right after the application's interface loads:

```
class GameViewController: UIViewController {
    override func viewDidLoad() {
        super.viewDidLoad()
        if let scene = GameScene.unarchiveFromFile("GameScene")
            as? GameScene {
            // Configure the view.
            let skView = self.view as SKView
            skView.showsFPS = false
            scene.size = skView.bounds.size
            skView.showsNodeCount = false

            /* SpriteKit applies additional optimizations
               to improve rendering performance */
            skView.ignoresSiblingOrder = true

            /* Set the scale mode to scale to fit the window */
            scene.scaleMode = .AspectFill

            skView.presentScene(scene)
        }
    }
     /* Several other methods */
}
```

A few built-in functions follow viewDidLoad. They control behavior like rotation and memory management. You should leave them in place and ignore them for now so that you can focus on the first method. The keyword override indicates that you're overriding a method of the same name in the parent class. In this case, the parent class of GameViewController is UIViewController. Calling super.viewDidLoad lets you keep the behavior of the parent controller's method and then extend it with your own logic. Don't forget to always call super. viewDidLoad().

The method's initial if statement loads a resource for the game scene. This relates to the file GameScene.swift, which you'll edit soon. The code within the if block changes two properties of the current view: showsFPS and showsNodeCount. You can set both properties to false because they're used primarily for debugging. Next, you adjust the scene's size to make it span the dimensions of skView.

Importing Image Assets

Your platform game uses images (pngs) to represent the ground, the player, and the player's obstacles. This chapter doesn't spend a lot of time on aesthetics because it isn't a design tutorial. Of course, you can feel free to polish up the graphics or create your own. Just make sure that the dimensions of your images are similar to those of the original pictures. Table 10.1 shows a detailed overview of the assets.

Table 10.1   **Image Assets**

Filename	Use in Game	Width	Height
hero.png	The player's avatar	60 px	60 px
play.png	Start button	272 px	114 px
bar.png	The ground	1344 px	64 px
block.png	Regular obstacle	60 px	60 px
block2.png	Tall obstacle	60 px	120 px

You need to import each of these assets into Xcode. To do this, you reveal the assets panel by selecting the Image Assets folder in the project tree. You can delete the spaceship image, which belongs to the default game. Then you start by adding the play button. Select the plus icon and then click New Image Set. Name the asset `play` and drag play.png onto the 1x tile in the main window. Repeat this process for each of the other images, naming each asset after the name of its corresponding file.

Here are the files:

- https://github.com/skipallmighty/Skiptaculous/blob/master/Skiptaculous/Images.xcassets/bar.imageset/bar.png

- https://github.com/skipallmighty/Skiptaculous/blob/master/Skiptaculous/Images.xcassets/block1.imageset/block.png

- https://github.com/skipallmighty/Skiptaculous/blob/master/Skiptaculous/Images.xcassets/block2.imageset/block2.png

- https://github.com/skipallmighty/Skiptaculous/blob/master/Skiptaculous/Images.xcassets/hero.imageset/hero.png

- https://github.com/skipallmighty/Skiptaculous/blob/master/Skiptaculous/Images.xcassets/play.imageset/play.png

The Start Screen

To build the tic-tac-toe game in Chapter 5, you imported image assets and referenced them in code. You'll create similar references for each of the assets that you imported in the previous section. You can begin with the play button. Define the resource as a constant in `GameScene.swift`, like this:

```
import SpriteKit

class GameScene: SKScene {

    let playButton = SKSpriteNode(imageNamed:"play")

    override func didMoveToView(view: SKView) {
        self.playButton.position = CGPointMake(CGRectGetMidX(self.frame),
                              CGRectGetMidY(self.frame))
        self.addChild(self.playButton)
        self.backgroundColor = UIColor(hex: 0x80D9FF)
    }

    override func touchesBegan(touches: NSSet, withEvent event: UIEvent) {
        /* Coming soon */
    }

    override func update(currentTime: CFTimeInterval) {
        /* Coming soon */
    }
}
```

The methods `touchesBegan` and `update` are listed to show how this class will eventually look, but you can focus only on `didMoveToView` for now. The code in this block executes whenever a player navigates to a view—in this case, the starting screen. Our first goal is to position the play button in the screen's center. You accomplish this by calling `CGPointMake`, which takes two `CGFloat`s as arguments.

Compared to regular floats, `CGFloat`s offer greater compatibility across operating systems. Keep in mind that `CGFloat` is a special type, and it isn't interchangeable with all floats in Swift. To make the button appear at center-screen, you need two `CGFloat`s that represent the horizontal and vertical centers of the game window. `CGRectGetMidX` and `CGRectGetMidY` are helpful built-in functions for finding the values.

Custom Colors

Now you have a play button, but the background is a boring white color. You can improve this by assigning a `UIColor` object to `self.backgroundColor`. Notice that you construct `UIColor` by using a hexadecimal value, also called a *hexcode*. By default, `UIColor` accepts color values in red-green-blue (RGB) form. To make the hexcode feature work, you add custom functionality to `UIColor`. Extending a class is fairly simple. Refer to your list of project files and right-click the Create New File button. Choose Swift as the file type and name the file `UIColorExtensions.swift`. Then add to it the following code:

```
import UIKit

extension UIColor {
    convenience init(hex: Int, alpha: CGFloat = 1.0) {
        let red = CGFloat((hex & 0xFF0000) >> 16) / 255.0
        let green = CGFloat((hex & 0xFF00) >> 8) / 255.0
        let blue = CGFloat((hex & 0xFF)) / 255.0
        self.init(red:red, green:green, blue:blue, alpha:alpha)
    }
}
```

During initialization, the class converts a hexcode to a set of RGB values. This code may be especially convenient to you if you're used to working with hexadecimals. In any case, it's useful to learn about extending classes. Extensions allow you to write your own methods and initializers (and other stuff) in an already-existing class, even classes like `String`, or `UIColor` as you saw here.

Handling Taps

Now that you've created and positioned the play button, you can detect when users tap it. Take another look at the empty `touchesBegan` method that you defined in `GameScene`. Fill it with the following code:

```
override func touchesBegan(touches: NSSet, withEvent event: UIEvent) {
    for touch: AnyObject in touches {
        let location = touch.locationInNode(self)
        if self.nodeAtPoint(location) == self.playButton {
            println("Play button pushed")
        }
    }
}
```

The opening `for` statement loops through all touch conditions to account for multitouch devices (as all touches will be sent in an array-like structure to this loop). When the player touches any part of the frame, the code finds the tap coordinates and stores them in `location`. Then you determine what object, if any, exists beneath the tap location. In this game, only the play button should start the game. The `if` statement enforces this rule by making sure an object coincides with the tap location and the object is the play button. You can preview the app to see your changes. If your code is working correctly, you should see the results of the `println` each time you tap the play button.

Dangerous Ground

If printing text brought you to the edge of your seat, hang on tightly. Things will get more exciting when you let players actually start the game. At this point, you should add a file named `PlayScene.swift` to your project. Just as `GameScene` contains logic for the start screen, `PlayScene` is in charge of the game's main play area. The barebones class should look like this:

```
import SpriteKit

class PlayScene: SKScene {
    override func didMoveToView(view: SKView!) {
        self.backgroundColor = UIColor(hex: 0x80D9FF)
    }
}
```

After you import SpriteKit, you define `PlayScene` as a child class of `SKScene`. The `didMoveToView` method is just like the one in `GameScene`. It fires when the player navigates to the view. You set the arena's background color and add a `print` statement only to establish that the class works. Preview the app, and you should notice that the play button still doesn't do anything. That's because you need to create a link between `GameScene` and `PlayScene`. Return to `GameScene` and update the `touchesBegan` method, like this:

```
override func touchesBegan(touches: NSSet, withEvent event: UIEvent) {
    for touch: AnyObject in touches {
        let location = touch.locationInNode(self)
        if self.nodeAtPoint(location) == self.playButton {
            var scene = PlayScene(size: self.size)
            let skView = self.view as SKView
            skView.ignoresSiblingOrder = true
            scene.scaleMode = .ResizeFill
            scene.size = skView.bounds.size
            skView.presentScene(scene)
        }
    }
}
```

The code now includes a reference to `PlayScene`. Passing `self.size` as an argument indicates that `PlayScene` should be the same size as `GameScene`. You use `as` to reference the current view because you know that `self.view` will always be an instance of `SKView`. Switching `ignoresSiblingOrder` to `true` lets SpriteKit perform extra optimizations. While this setting works for most projects, it may not be ideal for games that involve a lot of complex overlapping nodes. After scaling and sizing the main scene, you show it to the player by using `presentScene`.

Positioning Obstacles

The game's foundation is complete. You have created views for the start screen and the main play area, and you have imported all the image assets. Now you can weave the graphics into your views. First, you should add the ground. The player's avatar would drop into a blue abyss without it, and no one wants that. You can associate this node with the bar.png graphic. If you haven't imported this picture, please refer to the "Importing Image Assets" section, earlier in this chapter. After the asset is ready, position it in `PlayScene`, like this:

```
override func didMoveToView(view: SKView!) {
    self.backgroundColor = UIColor(hex: 0x80D9FF)
    self.runningBar.anchorPoint = CGPointMake(0, 0.5)
    self.runningBar.position = CGPointMake(
        CGRectGetMinX(self.frame),
        CGRectGetMinY(self.frame) + (self.runningBar.size.height / 2))
}
```

The runningBar constant is an SKSpriteNode that references bar.png. Knowing that the bar will serve as a ground surface, you should position it so it stretches along the bottom of the screen. By default, the position of every sprite is relative to the anchor point you set for the scene, but you can change any element's anchor point (including the main scene). You set the ground's anchorPoint to (0, 0.5). This point represents the left edge on the x coordinate and the middle for the y coordinate. In SpriteKit's coordinate system, (0,0) represents the bottom-left corner, and (1,1) represents the top-right corner. Given this, you can probably figure out that (0, 0.5) refers to a spot on the far left, halfway between the top and bottom of the frame (see Figure 10.3).

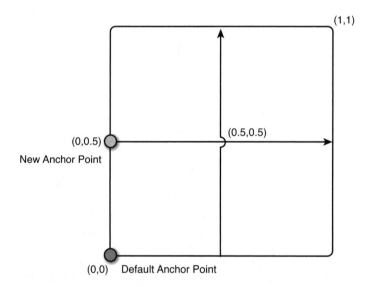

Figure 10.3   The coordinate system in SpriteKit and the changes we made.

To position the bar relative to the anchor point, you create another point by using CGMake. The first argument represents the bar's spot on the X axis. It should always appear on the far left of the frame. You can find this position by passing self.frame to CGRectGetMinX. Note that in this case, the function always returns a zero. While you could replace it with a hard-coded zero, the change might make the intent of your code less obvious. The performance gains would be minimal, too, because `didMoveToView` isn't called frequently.

You call `CGRectGetMinY` in a similar fashion to get the frame's bottom. There's just one problem: No one will see the ground if the top of bar.png begins at the bottom of the frame. The code makes the bar visible by adding half of its height to its position. Every `SKSpriteNode` contains a struct called `size`, which includes its width and height.

Moving Obstacles

Preview the app, and you should see a striped ground. That's nice, but the stripes are stationary. Your hero deserves a more action-packed environment. To make the stripes whoosh to the left by changing the bar's position each frame, add the following code to the `update` method in `PlayScene`:

```
override func update(currentTime: NSTimeInterval) {
    if self.runningBar.position.x <= maxBarX {
        self.runningBar.position.x = self.origRunningBarPositionX
    }

    //move the ground
    runningBar.position.x -= CGFloat(self.groundSpeed)
}
```

The bar.png graphic is wider than the frame so you we can move it to the left without exposing any white space. Just as the bar is sliding out of frame, the game resets its position. There isn't a noticeable jump-cut when the position shifts because the picture is made up of a repeating texture. You have to store the bar's original position in `origRunningBarPositionX` to reset it later. The `if` statement dictates that if the bar passes a horizontal threshold, you should push it back to its original place and continue the animation seamlessly.

The threshold represented by `maxBarX` is equal to the bar's width minus the frame's width. As long as the bar hasn't surpassed the limit, you can move it according to the distance defined in `groundSpeed`. If five pixels seems like a small distance, remember that the code in `update` executes on every frame (60 times a second). When you preview the app, prepare to be amazed by an infinitely scrolling bar, as shown in Figure 10.4.

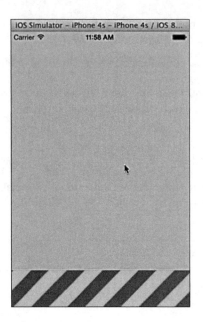

Figure 10.4   The ground in motion.

A Hero to the Rescue

The hero finally has a chance to stand his or her ground. It's time to create the player. Start by creating a variable "hero." This `SKSpriteNode` will reference the hero.png graphic that you imported earlier in this chapter. To position the circle above the platform, add a few lines to the `didMoveToView` method:

```
override func didMoveToView(view: SKView!) {
    self.backgroundColor = UIColor(hex: 0x80D9FF)

    self.runningBar.anchorPoint = CGPointMake(0, 0.5)
    self.runningBar.position = CGPointMake(
        CGRectGetMinX(self.frame),
        CGRectGetMinY(self.frame) + (self.runningBar.size.height / 2))
    self.origRunningBarPositionX = self.runningBar.position.x
    self.maxBarX = self.runningBar.size.width - self.frame.size.width
    self.maxBarX *= -1

    self.heroBaseline = self.runningBar.position.y +
        (self.runningBar.size.height / 2) + (self.hero.size.height / 2)
```

```
self.hero.position = CGPointMake(CGRectGetMinX(self.frame) +
    self.hero.size.width +        (self.hero.size.width / 4),
    self.heroBaseline)

self.addChild(self.runningBar)
self.addChild(self.hero)
}
```

Take a look at `self.hero.position` to see where the hero will end up. The first argument that you pass to `CGPointMake` is an X coordinate based on several factors. First, you find the position of the frame's left edge and add to it the hero's width. This positions the hero flush against the left-hand side of the screen. Adding another number—the hero's width divided by 4—provides some padding. Now refer to the second argument of `CGPointMake`. This Y coordinate is based on `heroBaseline`. Your calculation takes into account the bar's initial height and then adjusts for anchor points. To better understand how anchor points work, experiment with deleting the second and third numbers added to `heroBaseline`. Notice that the hero falls short of the bar's top edge. When you're done experimenting, make sure to restore the variable's original value.

Rotating Nodes

Now the hero stands in the right spot, but he or she looks boring in contrast to the exciting animated ground. Instead of making the sphere stationary, how about if you roll it over the striped bar? You can create this effect by rotating the player's avatar on each frame. Add the following code to the `update` method of `PlayScene`:

```
//rotate the hero
var degreeRotation = CDouble(self.groundSpeed) * M_PI / 180
self.hero.zRotation -= CGFloat(degreeRotation)
```

You have to define the `groundSpeed` constant, too. Write it as an integer-type property of `PlayScene`. The ground speed indicates how many degrees the sphere should rotate per frame. Converting the degrees to radians requires a bit of math. We play around with numbers until the hero rotates at the same speed as the ground. After you cast the integer as a `CDouble`, multiply it by pi and divide the product by 180. Rotate the hero by passing the radian value to the hero's `zRotation` property. Notice that you perform a type conversion on the radian because `zRotation` expects a `CGFloat`. Click Preview, and you should see the avatar spinning at a moderate pace (see Figure 10.5). As an experiment, you can tweak the ground speed to turn your character into a sloth or a speed demon.

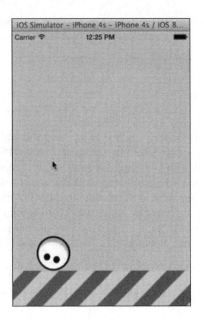

Figure 10.5   Hero is rolling.

Bar Hopping

Now that the hero is animated, you can make him or her jump on command. You start by
defining a few physics properties, such as a velocity and gravity. If you're not into math, don't
worry. The calculations involve basic addition and subtraction. Simply change the hero's velocity on every frame and during touch events, like this:

```
override func touchesBegan(touches: NSSet!, withEvent event: UIEvent!) {
    if self.onGround {
        self.velocityY = -18.0
        self.onGround = false
    }
}
override func touchesEnded(touches: NSSet!, withEvent event: UIEvent!) {
    if self.velocityY < -9.0 {
        self.velocityY = -9.0
    }
}
override func update(currentTime: NSTimeInterval) {
    //jump
    self.velocityY += self.gravity
    self.hero.position.y -= velocityY
```

```
    if self.hero.position.y < self.heroBaseline {
        self.hero.position.y = self.heroBaseline
        velocityY = 0.0
        self.onGround = true
    }
    /* Other code related to hero rotation */
}
```

The code overrides the `touchesBegan` method to detect when and where a player taps. You ensure that `self.onGround` equals `true` to prevent the player from jumping while he or she is already airborne. If consecutive jumps were allowed, players could fly into the clouds similar to Mario when he has his cape or raccoon tail (depending on your age and your desired level of nostalgia).

The variable `velocityY` determines how quickly (and ultimately how high) the player ascends. If the character is on the ground when a tap begins, you want to set the velocity to `-18`. If the touch event ends quickly, you want to set the velocity to `-9`. Changing the velocity at these points in the code affects the jumping behavior. The longer a player taps, the farther he or she leaps. Eventually, the avatar must return to Earth. That's where the `gravity` constant comes into play.

The `update` method subtracts `0.2` from `velocityY` on each frame. Just as the player shouldn't soar unrealistically, you don't want him or her to crash through the ground. Each time `update` is called, an `if` statement ensures that the player's vertical position never drops below `heroBaseline`. When the velocity gets too low, you will revert it to `0.0` and make `onGround` equal `true`.

Preview the app, and you should see your avatar leap every time you tap. You can experiment with tapping softly and holding down your finger to see how the actions produce different jumping effects. Changing gravity and velocity can affect the game's difficulty, too. You'll see why in the next section, when you work with barriers.

Enemies in Motion

In this game, barriers create a sense of danger. If the player collides with one of the block graphics, he or she bites the dust. The score display introduced later in this chapter rewards players each time they vault over an obstacle. Let's take an inventory of the graphic assets that you imported earlier. The `block1` picture is easy to vault because its height matches that of the avatar. The `block2` image offers a tougher challenge because it's twice as tall as the hero. You define both of them as properties of `PlayScene`:

```
let block1 = SKSpriteNode(imageNamed:"block1")
let block2 = SKSpriteNode(imageNamed:"block2")
```

After defining the blocks as `SKSpriteNodes`, you need to set their positions. You want the barriers to spawn on the ground and slightly beyond the screen's right edge. They'll eventually scroll from right to left. Keep in mind that the objects are positioned relative to their middle, or center, points. Because `block1` is equal in height to the avatar, you can position it vertically, using the same `heroBaseline` property. Positioning `block2` involves one extra step. You add `block2`'s height to `heroBaseline` to account for `block2` being taller than the player. This is all you need to do for the vertical (Y) positioning. To place the obstacles along the X axis, you call `CGRectGetMinX`, which returns the position of the screen's right edge, and add the block's width to it. When you're done positioning the blocks, remember to call `addChild` to attach them to the view:

```
self.block1.position = CGPointMake(CGRectGetMaxX(self.frame) +
        self.block1.size.width, self.heroBaseline)
self.block2.position = CGPointMake(CGRectGetMaxX(self.frame) +
        self.block2.size.width, self.heroBaseline +
        (self.block1.size.height / 2))
```

Elements of Chance

After you position the obstacles, you can make them spawn during gameplay. To do this, you need to write a few blocks of code. You'll create a class for keeping tabs on the status of a block, a dictionary in which to store all the blocks, and a method to make things happen randomly. Let's take it one step at a time and focus on the method for randomness. To keep the player on his or her toes, you want an obstacle to spawn at a random interval of 50 to 200 frames. You need to create a `random` method to generate numbers within this range:

```
func random() -> UInt32 {
    var range = UInt32(50)..<UInt32(200)
    return range.startIndex + arc4random_uniform(range.endIndex - range.startIndex + 1)
}
```

This code represents the frame range as an array of `UInt32` numbers. The built-in `arc4random_uniform` method spits out an integer between 50 and 200. Of course, this simple random number method does little on its own. The method's role will become clearer as you move on to tracking obstacles.

Tracking a Brick

To keep tabs on all the blocks, you need to create a dictionary named `blockStatuses`:

```
var blockStatuses:Dictionary<String,BlockStatus> = [:]
```

The `blockStatuses` dictionary consists of strings and a class called `BlockStatus`, which you define by adding a new file named `BlockStatus.swift` to your project and filling it with the following code:

```
import Foundation

class BlockStatus {
    var isRunning = false
```

```
var timeGapForNextRun = UInt32(0)
var currentInterval = UInt32(0)
init(isRunning:Bool, timeGapForNextRun:UInt32, currentInterval:UInt32) {
    self.isRunning = isRunning
    self.timeGapForNextRun = timeGapForNextRun
    self.currentInterval = currentInterval
}

func shouldRunBlock() -> Bool {
    return self.currentInterval > self.timeGapForNextRun
}
}
```

This class is short and sweet. It includes a few simple `Bool`s to describe the status of an obstacle. The `isRunning` property is `true` while the block is an active barrier that's visible to the player. `timeGapForNextRun` describes how long the block should wait before spawning. You need a measure of time to go along with the variable. `currentInterval` serves this purpose, telling how many frames have elapsed. By using these `Bool`s in combination with `shouldRunBlock`, it's easy to determine when a block should pop into the player's path.

Tracking All Blocks

Your next task is to fill the `blockStatuses` dictionary with instances of `BlockStatus`. First, you assign a `name` property to the `SKSpriteNode` references. This allows you to reference the nodes in a more succinct and convenient way:

```
self.block1.name = "block1"
self.block2.name = "block2"
```

Now you can instantiate `BlockStatus` for `block1` and `block2`, using the name of each block as a key:

```
blockStatuses["block1"] = BlockStatus(isRunning: false,
        timeGapForNextRun: random(), currentInterval: UInt32(0))
blockStatuses["block2"] = BlockStatus(isRunning: false,
        timeGapForNextRun: random(), currentInterval: UInt32(0))
```

The instances are nearly identical. You set `isRunning` to `false` and `currentInterval` to `0` to specify that the blocks aren't running, and they haven't spent time on the screen. The only difference is in `timeGapForNextRun`. The `random` method will almost always pass different integers to `BlockStatus`. Of course, the function could return the same number twice, but that's unlikely.

Spawned Obstacles

If you're ready to put your spawning logic to the test, you can move on to the `update` function. Your next challenge will to be hurl spawned obstacles toward the player. At the bottom of `update`, you call a method named `blockRunner`. The `blockRunner` function includes a few variables that are defined outside its immediate scope, as properties of `PlayScene`:

```
var blockMaxX = CGFloat(0)
var origBlockPositionX = CGFloat(0)
var score = 0
let scoreText = SKLabelNode(fontNamed: "Chalkduster")
```

Don't worry if you're not sure about the purpose of these variables. We'll soon discuss how they fit into the game. For now, let's talk about their structure and what they represent at a high level. The `blockMaxX` float is a horizontal cut-off point. When obstacles scroll from right to left, `blockMaxX` determines the point at which they vanish. After blocks disappear, the game must restore their original position. It uses `origBlockPositionX` to remember where the blocks were first situated. The `scoreText` property, which is of type `SKLabelNode`, displays the player's score. You can construct it using any font that's available to SpriteKit. In this case, go with Chalkduster because it has a game-like aesthetic. Use `CGGetMidX` and `CGGetMidY` to put the node center-screen.

Generating Barriers

You've already created the only external variables on which `blockRunner` depends. Now you can jump into the function itself:

```
func blockRunner() {
        for(block, blockStatus) in self.blockStatuses {
            var thisBlock = self.childNodeWithName(block)
            if blockStatus.shouldRunBlock() {
                blockStatus.timeGapForNextRun = random()
                blockStatus.currentInterval = 0
                blockStatus.isRunning = true
        }

            if blockStatus.isRunning {
                if thisBlock.position.x > blockMaxX {
                    thisBlock.position.x -= CGFloat(self.groundSpeed)
                }else {
                    thisBlock.position.x = self.origBlockPositionX
                    blockStatus.isRunning = false
                    self.score++
                    if ((self.score % 5) == 0) {
                        self.groundSpeed++
                    }
                    self.scoreText.text = String(self.score)
```

```
        }
    }else {
        blockStatus.currentInterval++
    }
  }
}
```

First, `blockRunner` loops through the dictionary of block statuses. It uses the native `child-NodeWithName` function to find the `SKSpriteNode` associated with each block. If it's time for a block to run, specify a new random spawn time and make the running status equal to `true`. If a block is already running, adjust its position. Pull the node farther left on each frame until it disappears from view. You can tweak `groundSpeed` to change how fast the obstacle travels.

After a node disappears from view on the left side, transport it back to its original position. This movement is invisible to the player, but it's how you prepare the block for its next run. Set `isRunning` to `false` to acknowledge that although the obstacle had a good run, its time in the spotlight is finished. If the block passed without incident, you should reward the player for a successful leap. Increment the `score` variable by 1.

Hardcore Mode

Players will eventually become familiar with the speed of the obstacles. With a bit of practice, they'll figure out the timing and rack up dozens of points. You want to provide more a challenge. For every 5 points a player scores, you should add 1 to the `groundSpeed`. The modulus operator provides a convenient way to keep count:

```
if ((self.score % 5) == 0) {
    self.groundSpeed++
}
```

Reading aloud, you can pronounce the percentage sign as "modulo" or use the colloquial term "mod." In this case, `score` mod 5 returns a 0 only when `score` is a multiple of 5. After you update the integer, display it by updating the `text` property of `self.scoreText`.

There's one final task to accomplish in the `blockRunner` method. You've handled the case of a block that's running, but there's no logic for blocks in which `isRunning` is `false`. Remember that the `BlockStatus` class waits for permission to spawn an obstacle. The class expects its `currentInterval` property to match `timeGapForNextRun`, its randomly generated waiting time. If a block isn't running, you need to increment `currentInterval` so that the block eventually spawns. The last `else` statement in `blockRunner` accomplishes this.

Smashing Physics

Your game has come a long way! Preview the app, and you should see barriers whizzing toward the player. The hero can jump in different ways to avoid collisions, and the ground moves faster as time progresses. The last order of business is to detect collisions between the player and the barriers. SpriteKit can handle much of the collision detection for us. You just have to tell it which objects should collide and when a collision should occur.

You need to create an `enum` for `PlayScene`, just above the `didMoveToView` method. You'll use this identify the hero and barrier objects for the purposes of collision detection:

```
enum ColliderType:UInt32 {
    case Hero = 1
    case Block = 2
}
```

Invisible Cages

Now you can tell SpriteKit to watch for collisions related to the hero. The key is to apply a physics body to the node. If you've created games before, you may be familiar with physics bodies. They're like invisible cages that wrap around game objects. The "cages" are typically made up of a simpler shape than the objects that they enclose. It's much easier for computers to process a shape that has fewer points. Think of scuba diving as an analogy: You step into a metal cage that detects collisions between you and a shark. It would be time-consuming and unnecessary (not to mention terrifying) to build a cage that conformed exactly to the shape of your body. There's one important caveat about this analogy: Although real-life cages are often box shaped, a physics body may conform to any simpler shape. In this case, it will take the form of a circle.

Here's how you place the circular physics body around the hero:

```
        self.hero.physicsBody = SKPhysicsBody(circleOfRadius:
            CGFloat(self.hero.size.width / 2))
        self.hero.physicsBody.affectedByGravity = false
        self.hero.physicsBody.categoryBitMask = ColliderType.Hero.toRaw()
        self.hero.physicsBody.contactTestBitMask = ColliderType.Block.toRaw()
        self.hero.physicsBody.collisionBitMask = ColliderType.Block.toRaw()
```

This code first creates an instance of `SKPhysicsBody`. Using `circleOfRadius`, you specify that the "cage" around the hero should be circle shaped. The next setting, `affectedByGrav-ity`, controls whether SpriteKit applies gravity to the object. You can make the attribute `false` because you've already handled gravity, and extra gravity could make the player break through the ground. The next few properties affect when and how collisions take place. SpriteKit uses `categoryBitMask` to identify the hero's physics body. You can pass it a value of 1, represent-ing the player, as defined in the `enum` for `ColliderType`. Similarly, you set `collisionBitMask` and `contactTestBitMask` to the numeric values for blocks that you defined in `ColliderType`. This means that the block should stop the hero from moving and trigger a collision event.

Now you can define physics bodies for the two block objects. The process is nearly the same, except the roles are reversed: Blocks should detect collisions with the hero. Another difference is that a property called `dynamic` must be set to `false`. A dynamic physics body is one that doesn't move during collisions. On the other hand, `static` bodies can displace each other. The game *Angry Birds*, for example, features both static and dynamic bodies. Birds cause other birds to bounce, but no creatures can move the ground by bumping into it. Taking these minor changes into account, you use this code for the blocks:

```
self.block1.physicsBody = SKPhysicsBody(rectangleOfSize:
        self.block1.size)
self.block1.physicsBody.dynamic = false
self.block1.physicsBody.categoryBitMask = ColliderType.Block.toRaw()
self.block1.physicsBody.contactTestBitMask = ColliderType.Hero.toRaw()
self.block1.physicsBody.collisionBitMask = ColliderType.Hero.toRaw()

self.block2.physicsBody = SKPhysicsBody(rectangleOfSize:
        self.block1.size)
self.block2.physicsBody.dynamic = false
self.block2.physicsBody.categoryBitMask = ColliderType.Block.toRaw()
self.block2.physicsBody.contactTestBitMask = ColliderType.Hero.toRaw()
self.block2.physicsBody.collisionBitMask = ColliderType.Hero.toRaw()
```

A Hero's Death

Before you test the collisions, you need to make two minor tweaks to the PlayScene class. First, make PlayScene inherit from the SKPhysicsBodyDelegate class. The inheritance gives your code access to SpriteKit's built-in methods for handling collisions:

```
class PlayScene: SKScene, SKPhysicsContactDelegate { ...
```

Second, inside didMoveToView, set a physics-related property called contactDelgate to equal PlayScene:

```
self.physicsWorld.contactDelegate = self
```

Now, when you preview the app, you'll have to be quick on your feet. If you don't vault the obstacles in time, they'll push you off the screen. That's mostly the behavior you want, except it's a little too forgiving. A collision should force the player to restart the game. Therefore, you need to add a method called didBeginContact to your PlayScene class:

```
func didBeginContact(contact:SKPhysicsContact) {
    died()
}
```

The built-in method fires whenever a collision occurs. Its main contact parameter includes useful information about which objects touched. For now, you can ignore this feature because the game doesn't need to know who crashed into whom. It just has to realize that a collision happened. In the event of a collision, it jumps to the died function, which you define like this:

```
func died() {
    if let scene = GameScene.unarchiveFromFile("GameScene") as? GameScene {
        let skView = self.view as SKView
        skView.ignoresSiblingOrder = true
        scene.size = skView.bounds.size
```

```
        scene.scaleMode = .AspectFill
        skView.presentScene(scene)
    }
}
```

The `died` function is responsible for cutting short the action. It prepares and presents the `skView` for our initial start screen. The settings here closely resemble those in the `touches-Began` method.

Summary

In this chapter, you worked with SpriteKit, a powerful framework for building games in Swift. When it comes to customization, SpriteKit places you, the programmer, in the driver's seat. After you import graphics, you can make them available as `SKNode` objects in a game. SpriteKit lets you fine-tune almost any node property. In this chapter, you created a game in which you adjusted the positions, colors, and rotation settings of some nodes. You positioned the hero and barrier blocks flat against the ground to create an illusion of gravity. You used an instance of the `UIColor` class to make the background look like a blue sky.

Unlike the tic-tac-toe example from Chapter 5, this game involves multiple views: a start screen and a main play area. You've learned that SpriteKit's `SKView` class helps you to organize your code and transition between game areas. By extending the library's built-in event handlers, you now know how to make an avatar leap after a tap event. Some basic physics and collision detection give the game a more dynamic feel. Players can jump in different ways to avoid the obstacles whooshing toward them. A physics body can handle the grunt work of detecting collisions. You simply tell it what should happen after a crash.

In this chapter, you started with a blank canvas and produced an action-packed platform game in Swift. Your avatar can vault any obstacles that spawn in his or her path. This is a good metaphor for you as a Swift programmer!

11

Games with SceneKit

SceneKit is to 3D what SpriteKit is to 2D. If you get nothing else out of this chapter, get that!

When you first create a SceneKit app from scratch, if you press play, you have a working game. You get a little spaceship that you can tap, and it will light up. This is a big step forward from trying to create such things yourself in any sort of framework. When you first create a SceneKit project, you see code for animation and touch events. SceneKit also has fully featured ways of storing and playing with your assets. You can import special DAE files provided by your artist. Your artist can put cameras and lights and all the objects with their materials in a DAE file. Once you have that DAE file, you can fully control all those objects individually. You can rename them and move them around. 3D can be tricky, so it's awesome that you can enlist the help of a professional 3D artist to help you out. Your 3D artist won't necessarily know about game making, but he or she will know about design and what looks good. SceneKit allows you to work together with an artist (or by yourself, or start from scratch).

There are a couple of terms you need to know before you start using SceneKit so that you don't get confused. You'll learn those next, and you'll also learn how to export your files yourself from free 3D tools like Blender.

Creating DAE Files

SceneKit can help you work with an artist's assets, as long as that person works with a specific format: a DAE file, otherwise known as COLLADA. COLLADA is a ubiquitous and open format, and every 3D authoring tool has the ability to export it.

COLLADA files are written in XML. You could write one yourself, although it would take a very long time, and you don't really have to do that. 3D programs often have proprietary or incompatible formats, and 3D itself is very complex. COLLADA is really great because it provides an open format that guarantees the 3D to be the same, no matter what software is used.

Xcode can edit DAE files that are imported, and you can resave them. To get started, you export your 3D model from whatever tool you are using; a popular one is Blender. Blender is a free and open source 3D authoring tool. It has a solid learning curve, but after you learn it, you can create absolutely amazing things. When you open Blender, you see something like what Figure 11.1 shows.

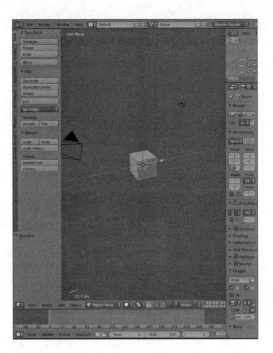

Figure 11.1   Blender's default view.

Blender has its own menu system, so you will use it to navigate instead of Mac's menu system. To export a COLLADA file, you select File > Export > Collada (default) .dae. Then you choose a location for your file. You might want to save your file to the desktop so click the Desktop directory. Figure 11.2 shows the save dialog.

| /Users/skipwilson/Desktop/ | Export COLLADA |
| untitled.dae | Cancel |

Figure 11.2   The save screen in Blender.

You can change the name of your file from "untitled.dae" to whatever you want. Note that COLLADA files cannot store image textures themselves. You'll have to grab them separately and often add the textures yourself in Xcode.

To see an example of a COLLADA file that my buddy Josh made for me, go to http://goo.gl/ nvZ69u. Go ahead and download it on your Mac. Then, when you click the file once to select it and press the spacebar to preview you it, you see the scene shown in Figure 11.3.

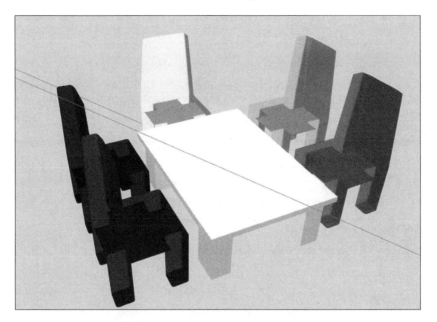

Figure 11.3   An awesome DAE file from Josh.

If your artist wants to use image-based textures, make sure you grab those image files from him or her separately. Notice that Josh did not use image-based textures, so the colors in his DAE file show up just fine.

> **Note**
>
> With image-based textures, you must make sure that your artist properly unwraps the textures for you before he or she exports them and hands them off to you. The artist needs to know how to do proper unwrapping. If he or she does not properly apply a texture to an object, you may wind up with some funky-looking textures.

Creating a New SceneKit Project

Now you are ready to import your DAE file into Xcode. In order to do this properly, you must create a new Xcode SceneKit project so you can import those files. Follow these steps:

1. Open Xcode and start a new project by selecting File > New > Project.

2. Choose the game template with the picture of the robot on the icon and click Next.

3. Name your project a name, such as SwiftStacker.

4. Make sure Language is set to Swift.

5. Make sure Game Technology is set to SceneKit.

6. Select iPad as the Device.

7. On the screen that allows you to save your new project, click Create.

8. When you get the list of initial project settings, select Landscape Right, as shown in Figure 11.4. (Because this is a game, you want to make sure that it is available in only one orientation.)

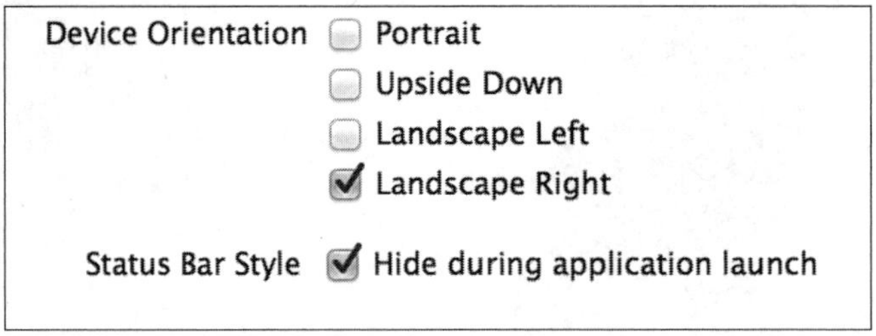

Figure 11.4   Orientation selection.

You are now ready to import your DAE file. Before you do, though, we need to take a look at the project structure and how Apple expects you to do things.

Your SceneKit Files

As you can see in Figure 11.5, these are the main components of your new SceneKit project:

- **`AppDelegate.swift`:** This is where you will get system-level updates, such as `applicationWillTerminate`, which is called when an application is about to terminate. At that time, you need to save all your data so you don't lose anything.

- **`art.scnassets`:** This is where Apple expects you to put all your DAE files. It's where you will put your assets in this chapter.

- **`GameViewController.swift`:** This is where Apple has written all of its game logic for the demo app. It connects to the `Main.storyboard` `SCNView` so that you can display your code on the screen. You can separate the game logic into more than one file. In fact, unless this game is a tiny itsy little one, then in order to create reusable assets, it is crucial that you organize your code well.

- **`Main.storyboard`:** This is where your one storyboard asset (`SCNView`) will sit. This asset will connect to `GameViewController`.

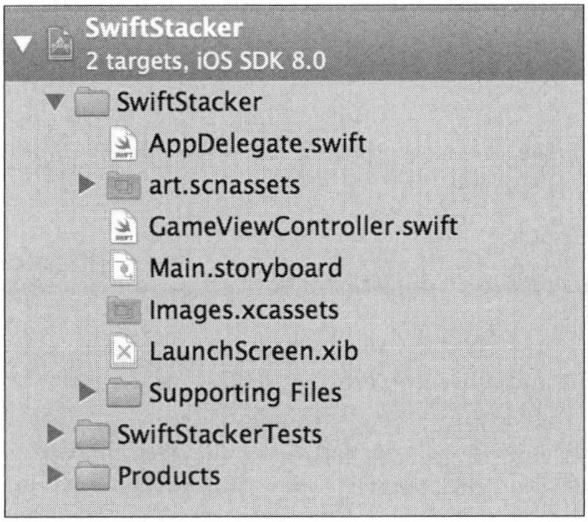

Figure 11.5   The new SceneKit project.

We don't need to talk about the rest of the files right now. You have your launch screen, which you can play around with, and you have Image.xcassets, which you can use if you decide to combine SpriteKit with SceneKit. You can create really nice GUIs for your SceneKit game by using SpriteKit on top of SceneKit.

Take a look at Main.storyboard, and you will notice that it is one screen with a giant black rectangle in the middle. Click that big black rectangle and select the Identity inspector. You should see that the class is set to SCNView.

Setting the Stage

SceneKit is set up much like a play in real life. When you go to see a play, from your seat you see a giant stage. This is represented in SceneKit by the SCNView. Currently there is nothing/no one on the stage, and there won't be until the play starts. When you run the application, the actors will enter the stage. In SceneKit, the actors are called *nodes*, and they are represented with the type SCNNode. All the SceneKit stuff starts with the prefix SCN. Everything that is added is of type SCNNode. For the most part, each camera, light, and other object on the stage is represented by a SCNNode. (Well, this isn't completely true, but it's a good way to think about it. In reality, you have the SCNCamera to represent a camera, which is not an SCNNode, but it gets attached to an SCNNode.)

Importing the Assets

Now you are ready to bring your COLLADA into Xcode. It's easiest if you open this directory in your Finder to do this:

1. Open Finder and navigate to your project. (For example, my project is located in `~/projects/SwiftStacker/`.)

2. Open the `SwiftStacker/art.scnassets/` directory.

3. Delete your current assets as you will not be using them for this tutorial.

4. Grab the DAE file from http://goo.gl/Bosq5l.

5. Move the DAE file and move into the `art.scnassets` directory.

Now you should be able to go into Xcode and view your asset. In Xcode, you can expand the `art.scnassets` directory and click on `stuff.dae`. You will get a nice menu that looks like the one shown in Figure 11.6.

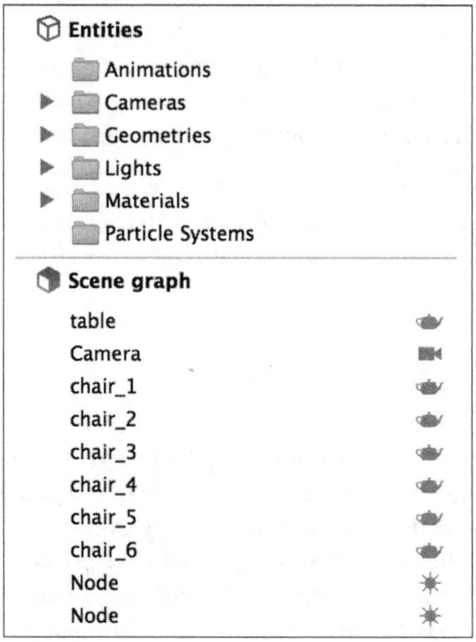

Figure 11.6   The Xcode 3D editor.

Notice that you have a list of all the objects in the scene. You have the table, camera, all the chairs, and two light nodes. The way you can tell that's a light is the symbol to the right is a little sparkly icon. You can rename a node by double-clicking its name. You will reference the names shown here in your code, so make sure these names are clear so you can easily associate them with their behavior.

This is a good time to talk about some 3D lingo. When you select one of the chairs, you will see its different properties pop up on the right side. If you click the Material inspector (the last icon on the right), you get info about the material.

Material Properties

When you open the Materials tab, you will see that it has lots of information on the different material properties. Let's talk about each one:

- **Diffuse:** This is the closest you can get to saying "the color of the object." More specifically it is the color the object reveals equally from all directions, from each point on the material's surface. A **diffuse map**, meaning an image, can be applied. This image will show directly on the surface of the object. Often, if it is a complex image, it must be mapped properly before being brought into Xcode.

- **Ambient:** This property makes it look as if light is hitting your object from all directions equally. For the ambient color of a material to be visible, you must have at least one light with a non-black ambient color. In the case of your app, that light type is SNCLightTypeAmbient.

- **Specular:** This is the shininess of your object. This property forms a glossy or bright highlight on the surface of an object. You must set a value of one of the lights to something other than black in order to see any shine. By default, the specular property is set to black, which means no shine, or dull. White appears as shiny. You can apply a specular map, meaning an image that tells the object where to appear shiny.

  When the specular map in Figure 11.7 is applied, the parts that get covered in black will become dull and non-shiny, and the parts covered in the white will become shiny.

Figure 11.7   A ridiculously simple specular map.

- **Normal:** This is a make-believe line that is perpendicular to the surface of a polygon. You can imagine that you have tons of normals on your object, all pointing in the direction of the average of the vertices of each triangle (see Figure 11.8).

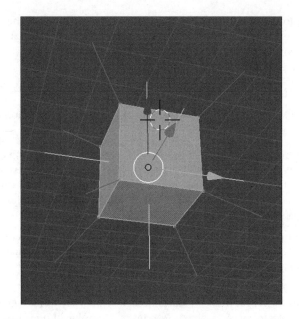

Figure 11.8   The little lines are the normals as seen from Blender.

In Figure 11.8, you can see the direction that the normals are pointing at the vertices of each triangle. You cannot directly see each triangle but they are there. You can change the direction of these normals all at once by using a **normal map** (otherwise known as a **bump map**). When the normal map is applied, you can fake the lighting of bumps and dents. You can use this to add a lot of detail without adding extra polygons. This is great for making a simple polygon appear as if it has much more detail.

For example, when the normal map shown in Figure 11.9 is applied to a sphere, it looks as shown in Figure 11.10.

Figure 11.9   A normal map to give your object the appearance of wrinkled paper or stucco.

Figure 11.10   This is the normal map from Figure 11.9 applied to a sphere.

- **Reflective:** Reflective causes an object to reflect the environment around it. You have to provide it with an image to reflect. SceneKit does not render real-time reflections of objects in the scene.

- **Transparent:** You use this property to provide a map that shows what part of the material will be transparent.

- **Emission:** You can provide SceneKit with an **emission map** (that is, an image that describes the emission). Emission maps tell SceneKit which parts of the object should glow with their own light source.

- **Multiply:** After you add all the needed properties of the materials listed previously, you can multiply the color of each represented pixel by the color of this property.

Making the Game

With your newfound knowledge you can create your initial scene. You can start by opening up `GameViewController.swift` and removing some of the default code. Rewrite `viewDidLoad` to look like this:

```
var scene:SCNScene!
override func viewDidLoad() {
    super.viewDidLoad()
    screenWidth = self.view.frame.size.width
    screenHeight = self.view.frame.size.height
    // create a new scene
    scene = SCNScene()
    // retrieve the SCNView
    scnView = self.view as SCNView
    // set the scene to the view
    scnView.scene = scene
    // allows the user to manipulate the camera
    scnView.allowsCameraControl = true
    // show statistics such as fps and timing information
    scnView.showsStatistics = true
    // configure the view
```

```
    scnView.backgroundColor = UIColor.whiteColor()
    //setup delegate
    scnView.delegate = self
    scnView.pointOfView = blockCam

    addFloor()
    addLevel()
    addBlock()
}
```

In your SceneKit app, the `viewDidLoad` function will get called when the view is ready. It's like saying creation is complete, and you can start programming. You'll always call the super `view-DidLoad` function so that the `UIViewController` that you inherit can do all the initial loading it needs to do. (Make sure you call that; if you don't, you might get some unexpected results.)

While you're here, you can add some global variables to the top of the code. (You won't use them all right away, but you might as well put them in so you won't get errors later.) Add these global variables right underneath the class declaration:

```
var floor:SCNNode!
var block:SCNNode!
var scene:SCNScene!
var scnView:SCNView!
var blockCam:SCNNode!
var screenWidth = CGFloat()
var screenHeight = CGFloat()
var blockCamRot:SCNVector4!
```

Then you load the DAE file by calling the `SCNScene` initializer, which takes the name of the COLLADA file as a named parameter.

You need to grab a reference to the view that you added in the storyboard. Every `UIViewController` has its own view that it can reference at any time. That's why it's called a view controller: It has a *view* that it is *controlling*. You can grab the view of your view controller by using `self.view`.

Now you can set the scene that your view will be displaying, by saying `scnView.scene` is equal to the scene you created above by file reference.

Then you set some basic properties of the scene, like `allowsCameraControl`, which gives you control over the camera. The really cool thing is that you do not have to create and position a camera yourself. You don't have to do this because my awesome artist Josh added his own camera in the DAE file. You can now take control of the camera that was added for you. You will be able to control its position, rotation, and so on.

You use `showsStatistics` to add some tiny little statistics to the bottom of the app specifically for debugging purposes. You need to remove those before you release your app to the general public. You also set the background color of the app to be white with `scnView.backgroundColor`.

At this point, you can run your app, and you should see it running on your iPad or the simulator.

> **Note**
>
> Often a SceneKit game may render pretty slowly on the simulator (even on a super-fast computer), but when you run it on an actual device, it runs very smoothly. You should test your SceneKit games on an actual device if you want realistic results. Of course, using the simulator will work, but you shouldn't be too shocked if it doesn't perform as fast as you expect it to.

At first your `LaunchScreen.xib` will run, showing the user a default launch screen that came with the app. Feel free to play around with the launch screen to make it perfect for this app. Then the app will load and show the scene. If yours doesn't load for some reason, check that the name you provided in the `art.scnassets` directory matches the name written in your code.

Adding a Floor

Now you can add a floor to your game. SceneKit has a special geometry class made just for this purpose. `SCNFloor` is an infinite floor to add to your scene. You can get the texture for this floor from http://goo.gl/8YTY5z.

Here's the code you add for the floor:

```
func addFloor() {
    var floorGeo = SCNFloor()
    floorGeo.reflectionFalloffEnd = 0
    floorGeo.reflectivity = 0

    floor = SCNNode()
    floor.geometry = floorGeo
    floor.geometry?.firstMaterial?.diffuse.contents = "art.scnassets/wood.png"
    floor.geometry?.firstMaterial?.locksAmbientWithDiffuse = true
    floor.geometry?.firstMaterial?.diffuse.wrapS = SCNWrapMode.Repeat
    floor.geometry?.firstMaterial?.diffuse.wrapT = SCNWrapMode.Repeat
    floor.geometry?.firstMaterial?.diffuse.mipFilter = SCNFilterMode.Linear

    floor.physicsBody = SCNPhysicsBody(type: SCNPhysicsBodyType.Static, shape: nil)
    floor.physicsBody!.restitution = 1.0

    scene.rootNode.addChildNode(floor)
}
```

This function is called from the `viewDidLoad` method. Here you create a new `SCNFloor`. This is the basic geometry model that the floor node will contain. Every `SCNNode` has its own geometry. You can create it on the fly, using a DAE file. You can also use one of the included classes. In this case, you are going to use the class that's available to you. When you do this, you can set the reflection level so that it's not reflective. Then you create the new floor node using a regular `SCNNode`. Take the geometry that you made and attach it to this node.

You set the floor to have a texture like the wood image. You do this by using diffuse, which is essentially what you would call the visible color or texture of your object. You set that wooden pattern to repeat on both the X and Y, otherwise known as `wrapS` and `wrapT`. You set a physics body for the floor. By creating a physics body and attaching it to the node itself, you automatically put physics into motion. There are three types of physics bodies that you should be concerned with. You use a static physics body here, which means that this is like an immovable object, just like a real floor is considered immovable. A ball that would balance against the floor would be considered movable, and that physics body would be set as dynamic. You set the restitution for the physics body to make the ground a little bit bouncy. Finally, you add the floor to the scene.

Adding the Level

Next, you will add a level that your ball or block or hero can run and play on. You are going to use a random function to place the blocks differently every time—similar to the way that *Minecraft* does it. This function is not nearly as complex as the *Minecraft* function. Here it is:

```
func addLevel() {
    var last:SCNNode!
    var blockWidth = CGFloat(2)
    var numberOfBlocks = 100
    for n in 1...numberOfBlocks {
        var chosenDirection = BlockDirection.getRandomDirection()
        var blockGeo = SCNBox(width: blockWidth, height: blockWidth, length:
          blockWidth, chamferRadius: 0)
        var block = SCNNode(geometry: blockGeo)
        var lastPos:SCNVector3 = SCNVector3(x: 0, y: 0, z: 0)
        if last != nil {
            lastPos = last.position
        }
        switch(chosenDirection){
            case .Top:
            block.position = SCNVector3(x: lastPos.x, y: lastPos.y + 1, z: lastPos.z)
            case .Right:
            block.position = SCNVector3(x: lastPos.x + 1, y: lastPos.y, z: lastPos.z)
            case .Left:
            block.position = SCNVector3(x: lastPos.x - 1, y: lastPos.y, z: lastPos.z)
            case .Front:
            block.position = SCNVector3(x: lastPos.x, y: lastPos.y, z: lastPos.z + 1)
            case .Back:
            block.position = SCNVector3(x: lastPos.x, y: lastPos.y, z: lastPos.z - 1)
        }
        last = block

        block.physicsBody = SCNPhysicsBody(type: SCNPhysicsBodyType.Static,
            shape: nil)
        if n == numberOfBlocks {
```

```
        // last block
        block.name = "GOAL"
    }
    self.scene.rootNode.addChildNode(block)
    }
}
```

You start the add-level function by creating a variable that will hold the last block placed. Obviously, this will be `nil` to start with. You set a variable for the block width, which you can play around with at your own convenience. You also set a variable that contains the number of blocks, which you can also play around with (and I encourage you to do so). You start a loop that goes from 1 to the number of blocks, which in this case is 100.

Placing Each Block

You want to place one block at a time in a loop. You get a random direction by creating an enumeration of different directions. To make this happen, place this code above your `view-DidLoad` function, inside the game class:

```
enum BlockDirection {
    case Left, Right, Front, Back, Top
    static func getRandomDirection() -> BlockDirection {
        var directions = [Left,Right,Front,Back,Top]
        var range = UInt32(0)..<UInt32(directions.count - 1)
        return directions[Int(range.startIndex + arc4random_uniform(range.endIndex -
            range.startIndex + 1))]
    }
}
```

This enumeration contains all the different directions in which you could place a block. You are placing a block in reference to the previous block. (You are not going to place any blocks on the bottom, so you leave out the bottom.) The static function grabs one random direction and returns it. It uses a special function `arc4random_uniform` that is especially fast. You can reuse this function for getting random numbers anytime you need it. Just replace the zero with your starting index.

You start by creating a box that the user can move around with his or her fingers. You create the geometry for that box as you did before, and then you add that geometry to a node. Because this is the first block in the loop, you set the last position so that you have one that is not `nil`.

You then create a `switch` statement based on the chosen direction that was given to you randomly. The five choices are all very similar except that each adds a block in the direction chosen, so that the block will be in a different position than the previous block. If, for example, top is chosen, a block will be placed above the previous block. If right is chosen, a block will be placed to the right of the previous block. If left is chosen, a block will be placed to the left of the previous block. You get the idea. `SCNVector3` is a special type for SceneKit—basically just an object with an X, Y, and Z points, with some special functionality for 3D. Finally, you save this last block that you just created so that the next time you know where the previous block is.

You add a physics body to this block to make it stationary, by setting the body type as static. You grab the last block and name it GOAL. You then add the block to the scene and then go through the loop again.

Creating a Hero

You can now add the custom functionality to create the hero that will move around the screen. You need some Objective-C code to make this work, so you will create a bridging header. Right-click your main project and add a new .h and .m file named SIMDHelper. Swift will ask whether you want to have it automatically create a bridging header file for you, and you should definitely say yes. When this file is created, some settings will be applied to your project so that the file is referenced properly.

Bridging the Gap to Objective-C

Swift allows you to bring in Objective-C code and use it directly in your Swift code. You can create classes, enums, and structs—and anything else you want. If something is not available in Swift that is available in Objective-C, you can easily make it available yourself by bridging. In this case, you want to add a low-level library called SIMD.h to your game. But before you can add it, you need to bridge it to Swift. In SIMDHelper.h, add the following content:

```
#import <Foundation/Foundation.h>
#import <SceneKit/SceneKit.h>
#import <simd/simd.h>

@interface SIMDHelper : NSObject
{

}

+ (SCNVector3) vector_maker:(float)followMeX :(float)followMeY
    :(float)followMeT :(SCNVector3)cameraSCNVector3 :(float)cameraDamping;

@end
```

Here you create a header file, which will allow you to use a type called vector_float3, which has not been implemented in Swift. You now need to write the function you created previously in your implementation file. Open SIMDHelper.m and add the following content:

```
#import "SIMDHelper.h"
#import <Foundation/Foundation.h>
#import <simd/simd.h>

@implementation SIMDHelper
```

```
+ (SCNVector3)vector_maker:(float)followMeX :(float)followMeY
  :(float)followMeT :(SCNVector3)cameraSCNVector3 :(float)cameraDamping {

    vector_float3 targetPos = {followMeX, followMeY, followMeT};
    vector_float3 cameraPos = SCNVector3ToFloat3(cameraSCNVector3);
    cameraPos = vector_mix(cameraPos, targetPos, (vector_float3)(cameraDamping));
    return SCNVector3FromFloat3(cameraPos);
}

@end
```

Here you create a target X, Y, and Z (labeled T for `vector_float3`) and convert it to `SCNVector3` by using a special function. In this case, you could write this entire thing in Swift if you were a little bit creative. But the point is that this code library was not available in Swift, and you are making it available through the bridging header. This code allows the camera to follow the hero.

Open up your bridging header file and add the following content if it doesn't already exist:

```
#import "SIMDHelper.h"
```

Swift looks at this file and imports all the headers in it. In your Swift code, you don't need to make any changes.

To recap, you imported some Objective-C files into Swift by using a bridging header. You needed three files in all. One is the regular header for your class, one is an implementation file that contains the actual function you want to run, and the third is the bridging header, which Swift will look at when it needs to pull in code from Objective-C. Now Swift will know that it should pull classes from that header file. You could fill this header file with as many classes as you need. The bridging between Objective-C and Swift that Apple does in order to make other classes available to you is probably done in a similar fashion. You really have a lot of control over what is available to you with this method. Even if everything is not yet implemented into Swift, you can implement it yourself.

Back to the Hero

You can now add code to add the hero to your game. The following code uses a block or a sphere, but you can use whatever you would like:

```
func addBlock() {
    var blockGeo = SCNBox(width: 1, height: 1, length: 1, chamferRadius: 0)
    block = SCNNode()
    block.geometry = blockGeo
    block.geometry?.firstMaterial?.diffuse.contents = UIColor.redColor()
    block.physicsBody = SCNPhysicsBody(type: SCNPhysicsBodyType.Dynamic,
        shape: SCNPhysicsShape(geometry: blockGeo, options: nil))
```

```
blockCam = SCNNode()
blockCam.position = SCNVector3Make(0,14,10);
blockCam.rotation = SCNVector4Make(Float(1.0), Float(0.0), Float(0.0),
    Float(-M_PI_4*0.75));
blockCamRot = blockCam.rotation
blockCam.camera = SCNCamera()
blockCam.camera!.xFov = 75
blockCam.camera!.zFar = 500

scene.rootNode.addChildNode(block)
scene.rootNode.addChildNode(blockCam)
}
```

Again, you start by creating the geometry, and you are free to use whatever geometry you like.
You then create the node and add the geometry to the node. You add some color to the block
or ball by setting the diffuse property. You tell Swift that you want this block to interact with
the physics world. You also tell Swift that it should be a dynamic body.

You then set up a camera to follow the hero. You set an initial position for the camera, and
you set a couple properties. xFov tells how far the camera can see on the X axis. (Fov stands for
field of vision.) zFar tells how far out you are able to see.

You finish up by adding the hero and the camera to the scene. Make sure you don't add your
camera to your hero. If you do, you are going to get a very shaky ride.

Adding the Controls

You can now add some rudimentary controls so that the hero is able to move around when a
player touches the screen. You could do this by using the accelerometer, and you could also do
it by using screen tapping or swiping. In this case, you will use screen tapping for now. Add the
following code to the bottom of your viewDidLoad method, and note that it includes some
commented code for handling swipes in two different directions:

```
let gestureRecognizers = NSMutableArray()
let tapGesture = UITapGestureRecognizer(target: self, action: "handleTap:")
tapGesture.numberOfTouchesRequired = 1
let twoTapGesture = UITapGestureRecognizer(target: self, action: "handleTwoTap:")
twoTapGesture.numberOfTouchesRequired = 2
//        let swipeLeftGesture = UISwipeGestureRecognizer(target: self,
    action: "handleSwipeLeft:")
//        swipeLeftGesture.direction = .Left
//
//        let swipeRightGesture = UISwipeGestureRecognizer(target: self,
    action: "handleSwipeRight:")
//        swipeRightGesture.direction = .Right
//
//        gestureRecognizers.addObject(swipeLeftGesture)
```

```
//        gestureRecognizers.addObject(swipeRightGesture)
gestureRecognizers.addObject(tapGesture)
gestureRecognizers.addObject(twoTapGesture)
scnView.gestureRecognizers = gestureRecognizers
```

Here you see how to add gesture recognizers to the app. You can see that I left in two gesture recognizers and commented out two of them. The way it works is you create the individual gesture recognizers themselves and add them to an array. You then take that entire array and set it as the set of gesture recognizers for the entire view. You have a single one-finger tap and a single two-finger tap set here. The way that you are able to set how many fingers are required for the tap is by setting the property of the gesture recognizer `numberOfTouchesRequired`. These will trigger only if the number of fingers set touch at the same time. One finger will move the hero, and two fingers will make the hero jump. Here's how you add those two functions to the code, along with the listeners for the swipe-left and swipe-right functions that you might choose to use later:

```
func handleSwipeLeft(gestureRecognizer:UIGestureRecognizer) {
}

func handleSwipeRight(gestureRecognizer:UIGestureRecognizer) {
}

func handleTap(gestureRecognize: UIGestureRecognizer) {
    moveBlock(gestureRecognizer: gestureRecognize)
}

func handleTwoTap(gestureRecognize: UIGestureRecognizer) {
    block.physicsBody?.applyForce(SCNVector3(x: 0, y: 4, z: 0), impulse: true)
}
```

The best way I've found to move a body is to apply a force to it. You don't want to change the velocity directly because you'll get a very jerky motion. If you just apply some sort of force to the object, though, it will figure out all the physics on its own. The tapping functionality is complicated, so you put it in its own function:

```
func moveBlock(#gestureRecognizer:UIGestureRecognizer) {
    let p = gestureRecognizer.locationInView(scnView)
    let halfScreenWidth = screenWidth / 2
    let halfScreenHeight = screenHeight / 2
    var directionX = (screenWidth/2) - p.x
    var directionY = (screenHeight/2) - p.y
    var perc = CGFloat()
    if directionX < 0 {
        directionX = fabs(directionX)
        perc = directionX / halfScreenWidth
        if directionY < 0 {
            directionY = fabs(directionY)
            perc = directionY / halfScreenHeight
```

```
            block.physicsBody?.applyForce(SCNVector3(x: 1, y: 0, z: 1),
                impulse: true)
        } else {
            block.physicsBody?.applyForce(SCNVector3(x: 1, y: 0, z: -1),
                impulse: true)
        }
    } else {
        if directionY < 0 {
            directionY = fabs(directionY)
            perc = directionY / halfScreenHeight
            block.physicsBody?.applyForce(SCNVector3(x: -1, y: 0, z: 1),
                impulse: true)
        } else {
            block.physicsBody?.applyForce(SCNVector3(x: -1, y: 0, z: -1),
                impulse: true)
        }
    }
}
}
```

This is just an implementation of moving the hero around. What you do first is get the point that the user tapped on the screen. You divide the screen into four sections, similar to folding a paper in half and then in half again. You will watch where the user clicks on the screen and move the hero in that direction. You get a percentage of how far the user clicked on that side so that you can move the hero further in that direction. If the direction X is less than zero, then you know that the user clicked on the left side. (Everything having to do with X is on the left and right sides.) So you can declare that the user clicked on the left side.

Within that left- and right-side functionality, you can make a decision about whether the user clicked on the top or the bottom of the left side or right side. So if the direction is less than zero, you know that the user clicked on the top half of the screen. You use the special little function fabs, which gets the absolute value of a float. The absolute value means that if the float is negative, it will be positive, and if it's positive, it will still be positive.

Now that you know the finer details of where the user clicked on the screen, you can get the percentage of how far the user is in that section of the screen and apply force to the object according to that direction. In the else section of the code, you check whether the user clicked on the other side of the screen, but everything else is the same. Figure 11.11 shows what your scene will look like.

Figure 11.11   Your SceneKit game.

Summary

In this chapter, you created a basic scene, and you can now move the hero around in it. You created a floor and a bunch of blocks that randomly generate, and you made it possible for the ball to jump off those blocks. You created an initial camera view, and you cast shadows and allowed physics to do its thing. If you had used a DAE file in this example, you could have utilized and controlled the artist's cameras and lighting.

SceneKit is a super-high-level framework that gives you control over a bunch of low-level features. The editor that comes with Xcode 6 can actually edit your files, which you can then resave and redistribute. It's not meant for heavy editing, but it is a very realistic option to use. You've seen that without writing much code at all, you can create a full-fledged game.

A physics library is completely built in to SceneKit and doesn't need any configuration at all. If you've ever worked with 3D in the past, you know how complicated it can be even to just set it up. 3D has a completely unique lingo, which brings a slight learning curve. Although the terminology can be very confusing, SceneKit is almost as easy to use as SpriteKit. It's almost exactly the same—but with one extra dimension. Thankfully, Apple takes care of all the memory management and garbage collection in Swift. You can write an entire game with fewer than 50 lines of code.

Blender is an easy-to-use 3D editing tool that you can get going on your own in a small amount of time. (Another tool you could use is SketchUp, which is even easier to use and can export DAE files.) Blender also has the levels of complexity you need built in, so there's no stopping you from making anything you want. The scene you created in this chapter is able to run at more than 40 frames a second. You could organize the game into multiple classes to make it more reusable.

12

Apps with UIKit

Apple has two major kits available in its library: UIKit and AppKit. AppKit is for desktop applications, and UIKit is for iOS applications. In this chapter you are going to explore UIKit and take a look at how to build some common applications.

UIKit has gotten much easier to use in this iteration of iOS. While you can write everything from scratch in code, it's much easier to use the storyboard. Thanks to the storyboard, things like size classes mixed with constraints make automatic layout of your application super easy. A lot of the applications that you see in the App Store and applications that you've used every day are built using these utilities. You can customize these UI tools as much as you need to.

In this chapter, you will learn about a couple of the most common tools and how to use them. Each tool is meant to be used in a specific way. This means that Apple expects you to write your code in a way that fits its design guidelines. At first, these coding guidelines might seem complicated, but you will eventually realize how nice it is to have a plan of attack for each situation that arises. Unlike with other frameworks, Apple has design guidelines that are meant to be followed. This doesn't mean you can't step outside those guidelines; in fact, doing so might be what makes your app unique. You can use these user interface designs to your advantage to build the app that you want, quickly and painlessly. The first couple times you create a table or a search, you might think about the complexities of this design. After doing it 30 or 40 times, you'll be able to do it with your eyes closed. And there's nothing wrong with creating a custom user interface that you feel is appropriate. Just don't use undocumented functions or Apple will probably reject your app.

Application Types

Each app gets a storyboard, which is named `main.storyboard`. This is basically a giant XML file that describes the app's layout. In this chapter, you'll learn how to implement these common user interface designs by using Swift. To see how it works, you need to create a new project by selecting File > New > Project. At this point, you should be presented with a screen that looks like the one shown in Figure 12.1. The following sections describe the application types shown in this figure.

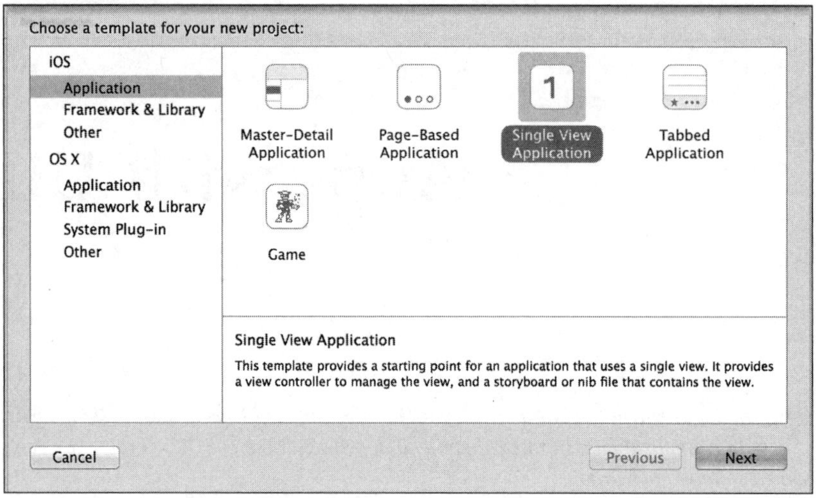

Figure 12.1   Choosing your application starting point.

Single-View Applications

When you start with a single-view application, Xcode starts you off with just a simple `UIView`, the most basic view available. A lot of other views inherit from this view. To choose this kind of application, click Single View Application and then click Next. Name your project single view, make sure Language is set to Swift, and make sure the Device is Universal. When you open the `Main.storyboard` file, you see the view shown in Figure 12.2.

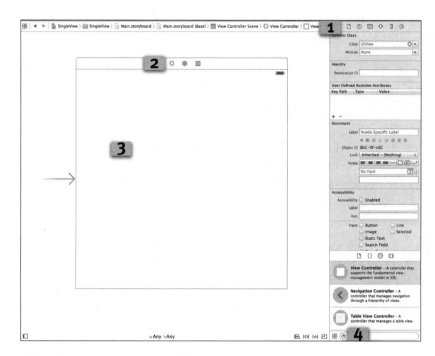

Figure 12.2   The `main.storyboard` GUI layout.

In Figure 12.2, note the couple of labels added to the storyboard:

1. In this sidebar area, you can make changes to things that are currently selected in the main area (#3). Most importantly, you have that toolbar of six icons (right next to the #1). I refer to this as the *sidebar toolbar*. Hover over each icon to see its name (currently the Identity inspector is selected).

2. Each view has an accompanying `ViewController` (which controls the view, as you would expect). This Swift file can also control the stuff on this screen. To select a `ViewController` and get options for its context in the sidebar area, click the little yellow icon with the white square in it (next to #2). I refer to this as the view controller button.

3. This is the view itself, which is currently just a plain view with nothing in it. Notice the arrow pointing at it on the left. This means that this is the first view. When your app starts, this is the first view that pops up.

4. This is the component area, where you can add more views by dragging them onto the screen as well as other user interface controls, like buttons and labels you want to put in your view.

To examine the classes this view is made of, click the view (#3 in Figure 12.2). It sometimes seems like nothing happens when you click the view, but don't worry: clicking really does select it. Now select the Identity inspector from the sidebar toolbar (the third icon from the left). You should see that the class for this view is a UIView (see Figure 12.3).

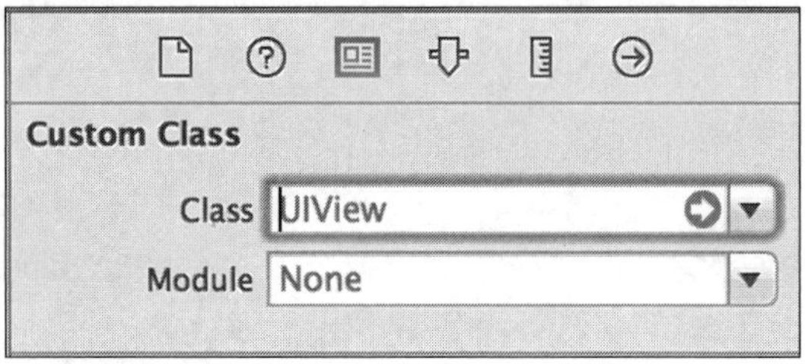

Figure 12.3   The Identity inspector.

This means that if you want to program things in Swift for this view, you will be dealing with the UIView class. In order to control UIView, you use a UIViewController. So you need to determine which UIViewController is currently controlling this UIView. Click on the view controller button (next to #2 in Figure 12.2). In the sidebar toolbar, make sure the Identity inspector is selected again. As shown in Figure 12.4, you see that the class assigned to the view controller is called ViewController.

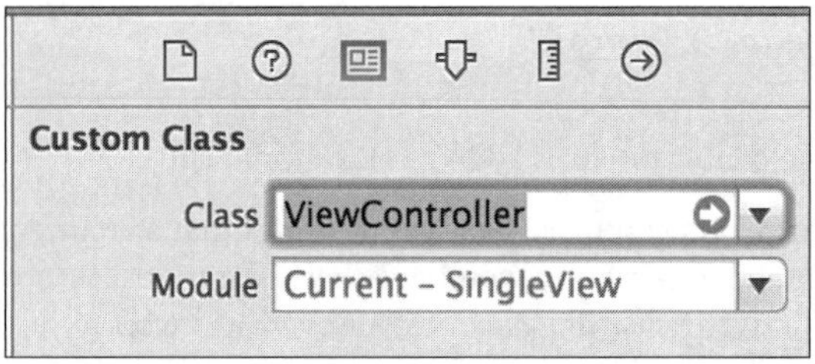

Figure 12.4   Renaming the class in the Identity inspector.

This class is currently in your project. If you look in your list of files, you will see a file called ViewController.swift. You can either open it there by clicking the filename or by clicking the arrow next to the word ViewController in the dialog shown in Figure 12.4. After you open the file using either method, you should notice that this class inherits from UIViewController. Now you know that if you want to control UIView by making your own view controller, you must create a class that inherits from UIViewController. You should see something like this:

```
class ViewController: UIViewController {
```

If you were to create a new file and in that file you created a class that inherited from `UIViewController`, then in that drop-down in Figure 12.4 you would see that class. You could then assign that custom class as the view controller for your view. Although Xcode automatically generates all the code you need to get your project started, you now know how to create a project from scratch.

> **Note**
>
> Don't forget that any changes you make in your storyboard must be saved, as the storyboard is just like any other regular file.

Go back to the storyboard and add a button on the screen. Go down to the section labeled #4 in Figure 12.2. In the search box, type the word `button`. When a button comes up for this search, you can drag it onto your view. If you hover the button around the center of the view, you should be able to get it locked in on center, both horizontally and vertically. (Note that this does not guarantee that your button will stay in the center when the device is rotated. You would need to add constraints in order for that to work.) After you place the button onto the screen, click the view controller button, and in the top-right corner (second from the left of six buttons) you should see a button that looks like a tuxedo (it may also be two circles in Yosemite (the new Apple operating system); either way it is called the assistant editor and it is second from the left). Click this button (see Figure 12.5).

Figure 12.5   The assistant editor is selected.

Clicking the tuxedo button brings up the code that accompanies your view controller. You should now have a split view of the storyboard and the `ViewController.swift` file. You want to be able to control the button that you created from the code. Therefore, you need to create a reference to the button in the code as well as an action for the button in the code. In order to do this, Control+drag the button from the storyboard over to the `ViewController.swift` file (see Figure 12.6).

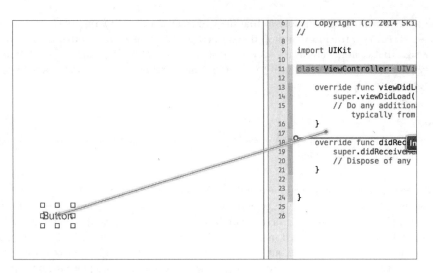

Figure 12.6   Creating a reference in the code by Control-dragging.

In the dialog that pops up, for Connection choose Action. This allows you to respond to the button being clicked by running your own function. In the Name field type `buttonClicked`. This will be the name of the function that Xcode will create. Click Connect. Xcode creates a function that looks like this:

```
@IBAction func ButtonClicked(sender: AnyObject) {
}
```

It's important to note that just because you created this function does not guarantee that everything is connected properly. If you did everything as instructed, of course it should work, but sometimes things get messed up when you experiment and don't do it right the first time. It's important to know for sure that things are either connected properly or not. So take a look: In the storyboard click the button to select it. In the sidebar toolbar, click the arrow button (the one farthest to the right) to show the Connections inspector. If you have the button selected, you can see all the events that should be triggered when that button is acted upon. You should see an event listed for Touch Up Inside (see Figure 12.7). If you want to cancel the connection, you can click the X in that area.

Figure 12.7   Viewing your connections.

This means that your button (when touched) is going to look for a method called button-Clicked. In the code, you can now respond to the button being clicked. For now you can just print something when the button gets clicked. Change your methods to look like this:

```
@IBAction func buttonClicked(sender: AnyObject) {
    println("Button was clicked!")
}
```

Now you can run the program and click the button. Try it to see if it works. When you run the program in your console, you will get the message from the function. The button is horribly positioned, however. You can quickly fix that by adding some constraints to the button.

Adding Constraints

By adding constraints, you allow the compiler to automatically calculate the position of your controls. When you first add constraints, the drawn line of the constraint may be orange, or it may be blue. It's important to know that when the line is orange, it means that you have not given Xcode enough information to calculate the constraint fully, and therefore it cannot properly position your item. It is not until your constraints turn blue that you can be sure that they are going to work.

To add a simple constraint to your button, Control+drag the button to the left and let go (in the whitespace area). A dialog appears, allowing you to choose a constraint. Choose Center Vertically in Container. You should now have an orange line going horizontally across the button. (Remember that orange means that the constraint is not totally set yet.) Add one more constraint by Control+dragging from the button up. A dialog appears, allowing you to choose a constraint. Choose Center Horizontally in Container. Your previous constraint should now turn blue, and you should have a new constraint going from top to bottom that is also blue.

You can now run your program once more, and the button should be perfectly centered.

Adding a New View

To improve your app, you can add another view that this view will transition to. Before you do anything else, though, change the label of the button to say Go. In your component search, look for and add two text fields and a label. Place the two text fields, spaced apart, below the Go button and place the label in the middle, with the text +. You can add a bunch of constraints to each item. You can see all the constraints added in Figure 12.8, as well as the layout on the right. You can add these constraints manually by Control+dragging from each item and choosing the constraint. If you resize anything after a constraint is applied, you must update the constraint. As soon as you resize, you see lines turn orange, which means you messed up the constraints, tsk tsk. If this is the case, you should see the icons in Figure 12.9 at the bottom of your storyboard. You can click the triangle (see Figure 12.8) and click Update Constraints. The other option is to click Update Frames to resize your item to match the constraints. When adding constraints, you can also highlight an item and click the second icon on the left (the square with two lines), and you can add individual constraints that way as well.

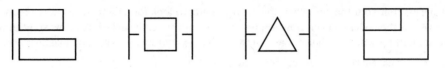

Figure 12.8   Constraint buttons in the Storyboard.

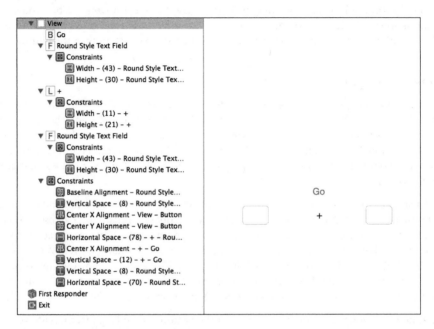

Figure 12.9   Constraint editing options; may also be hieroglyphics from the year 2000 B.C.

When you run the app and rotate the iPhone or iPad, these items should stay centered. You can add references to these text fields in your code. Control+drag from the first text field to the code. For Connection, choose Outlet. For Name, enter addFirst. Then you can click Connect. Do the same thing for the second text field, except name it addSecond. After you hook those up, you can change the contents of your button-click listener, like this:

```
IBAction func buttonClicked(sender: AnyObject) {
    println("Text1 \(addFirst.text) Text2 \(addSecond.text)")
}
```

Now you can get text out of the two text inputs. You can run this and give it a try.

Now you have a single view with input for the user and a button that responds to the user's input. Now you need to take the contents of those two inputs and add them together and display them on the next page. The first step is to add another view, so go into your component search area and type in `UIView`. You should see a view controller pop up in the search. Drag it onto your screen, to the right-hand side of the original view, as shown in Figure 12.10.

Figure 12.10   Adding a second view.

You can add a custom class to control this view individually. In your project navigator, add a new Swift file. In the new file dialog on the left-hand side, under iOS, choose Source, select New Swift File, and click Next. Name this file `DetailView.swift`. You can now create a detailed view that inherits from `UIViewController`. Add the following code to your detail view:

```
import UIKit
class DetailView: UIViewController {
}
```

After you create a detail view that inherits from the `UIViewController`, you can now have this code control the new view that you just created. Open your storyboard again and select the view controller button for that second view you just created. In the sidebar toolbar, make sure that the Identity inspector is selected, and for the class in the custom class, select the drop-down, where you should now see the new detail view as an option (see Figure 12.11).

Figure 12.11   Changing the class for the view in the storyboard.

Select the detail view, and if you still have the assistant editor button at the top selected, your detail view should now appear on the right-hand side of the split screen. You now have the detail view hooked up to your new view. Now you need to create a variable to store the answer to the addition in your first view. Add this variable to your detail view:

```
class DetailView: UIViewController {
    var total = 0
}
```

Now in your storyboard, select the first view, which should set your right-hand split screen to open up the `ViewController.swift` file. You need to create a segue from the first view to the second view. Control+drag from the Go button to the second view. When the dialog pops up, choose a show (that is, push) segue. You should now have the symbol shown in Figure 12.12 between your two views.

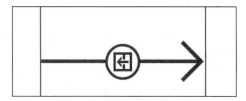

Figure 12.12   A push segue.

If you ran this now, it would work just fine because the segue is going to respond to the click of the button. However, you don't have any details on the second view yet. You also need to set details on the second view before the transition happens. In order to catch a segue before it happens and set some details, you can use this:

```
override func prepareForSegue(segue: UIStoryboardSegue, sender: AnyObject?)
```

This function returns the actual segue that is about to happen. Before the segue happens, you can set the total on the new view. Add this code to your view controller:

```
override func prepareForSegue(segue: UIStoryboardSegue, sender: AnyObject?) {
    var controller = segue.destinationViewController as DetailView
    controller.total = addFirst.text.toInt()! + addSecond.text.toInt()!
}
```

Here you are grabbing an instance of the controller that you are about to transition toward. You are also setting the total on that controller. All you have to do is add the two values from the text inputs together as integers. You are not really doing any error checking here.

Now you need to set a label on the second view so that you can show the total after it's set. Search for a label in the list of components on the bottom-right side. Add that label to the second view. Try to line it up so that it's horizontally and vertically centered. After you add the label, Control+drag the label to the left and add a Center Vertically in Container constraint.

Control+drag up from the label as well and add a Center Horizontally in Container constraint. Your two constraints should now be blue, which means you're good to go.

You need to create a reference for this label in the detail view. To do this, Control+drag from the storyboard's second view label to the detail view (see Figure 12.13). Try not to grab the constraints of the label at the same time. (It helps if you deselect the label first.)

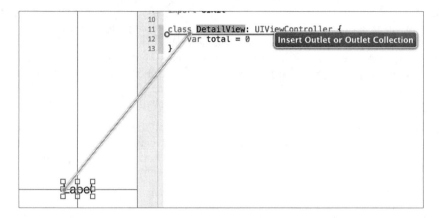

Figure 12.13   Adding an outlet for the label so you can change its text.

In the pop-up that appears, choose Outlet for Connection, name it `answerLabel`, and click Connect.

You need to add a function that gets called when the detail view is loaded. This is a perfect job for `viewDidLoad`. Add this code to your detail view:

```
override func viewDidLoad() {
    answerLabel.text = String(total)
}
```

Here you are setting the label to be what the total will be. The other view controller in `prepareForSegue` will set the total.

If you run the app, it should work. The total will come up on the second view. This process of creating segues and intersecting them before they arrive, while setting variables, is a very common way of doing things. You don't have to create segues programmatically; you let the storyboard do most of the work. For each view, you should create a new view controller file.

Loading a Table View

The small app you just created should give you an idea of how to structure much larger apps. If you give each view its own file, that separation of concerns will keep things loosely coupled.

This is an MVC (model view controller) without the model. When you're loading data for a table view, you must have a model because table views contain data.

We will now create another application from scratch. Create a new single-view project, with all the same settings as before. Choose File > New > Project, choose Single View Application, and give it a name. Create that project and save it. You should now have a blank single-view application with the first view set. Delete that first view by selecting the view controller button on that view and pressing the Delete key. In the search component area in the bottom-right corner, you should see a table view controller, which you can drag onto the screen. You no longer have a first view set, so you need to set the new table view controller as the first view. To do this, select the view controller button of the new table view that you've added, and in your sidebar toolbar area, make sure the Attributes inspector (the fourth button from the left) is selected. In the View Controller section, you should see the check box Is Initial View Controller. Select this check box, and you should get an arrow in front of your view.

A table view accepts data, so you should create a model for all that data. Pretend that your table is going to store a bunch of cars, and you want to create a structure that will hold one individual car. In your project, create a new file called `Car.swift`, with the following contents:

```
struct Car {
    var make:String
    var year:String
    var worth:Float
}
```

The view controller must inherit from `UITableViewController` in order to get all the benefits of the table that you are going to be controlling. This class needs to have a couple functions in order to work. You can add two of them right now:

```
override func numberOfSectionsInTableView(tableView: UITableView) -> Int {
    return 1
}
override func tableView(tableView: UITableView, cellForRowAtIndexPath
    indexPath: NSIndexPath) -> UITableViewCell {
    var cellIdentifier = "carCell"
}
```

Tables use cells to render information so you need to identify a cell that you are going to use in your table. So go back to the storyboard, and in the table view that you created, click once on the only cell in the table. Make sure in your sidebar toolbar that the Attributes inspector is selected. Change the Table View Cell Style setting from Custom to Subtitle, and name the cell identifier `carCell`. Now you can go back to your `tableView cellForRowAtIndex-Path`. You are telling the table view to use this `carCell` in the code. Now you can add some cars to a car array. You need to create a couple methods that the table needs, so rewrite your `ViewController.swift` like this:

```
override func viewDidLoad() {
    super.viewDidLoad()
    cars.append(Car(make: "Ford", year: "1954", worth: 2_000_000.0))
```

```
    cars.append(Car(make: "Mercedes", year: "2000", worth: 58_000.0))
    cars.append(Car(make: "Yugo", year: "1975", worth: 0.20))
    println(cars.count)
}

override func didReceiveMemoryWarning() {
    super.didReceiveMemoryWarning()
    // Dispose of any resources that can be re-created.
}

override func numberOfSectionsInTableView(tableView: UITableView) -> Int {
    return 1
}

override func tableView(tableView: UITableView, numberOfRowsInSection
    section: Int) -> Int {
    return cars.count
}

override func tableView(tableView: UITableView, cellForRowAtIndexPath
    indexPath: NSIndexPath) -> UITableViewCell {
    var cellIdentifier = "carCell"
    var cell:UITableViewCell = tableView.dequeueReusableCellWithIdentifier
        (cellIdentifier, forIndexPath:
    indexPath) as UITableViewCell
    cell.textLabel?.text = "\(cars[indexPath.row].year) -
        \(cars[indexPath.row].make)"
    cell.detailTextLabel?.text = "$\(cars[indexPath.row].worth)"
    return cell
}
```

Notice that every time you create a table, you need specific methods, in order, for the table function. You need at least need the following three methods:

- **override func tableView(tableView: UITableView, cellForRowAtIndexPath indexPath: NSIndexPath) -> UITableViewCell {:** This method tells Swift how to render each cell for the table. It will be sent an index path, which is the current row that it needs to render. In this case, you tell it to use the carCell cell that you created in the storyboard. In this function, you create a new reusable UITableViewCell. You assign the text to the cell. You also assign some detail text because you are using the subtitle cell. In the end, you must return the cell in order for the function to work properly.

- **override func tableView(tableView: UITableView, numberOfRowsInSection section: Int) -> Int {:** This method tells Swift how many rows will be in the table. You use the count of cars in the array. It's good to use a variable here because it may change later. If it does, you won't have to change this function, or write if statements; it will always work because the array count will fluctuate, and this method will be called whenever the table needs to be reloaded.

- **override func numberOfSectionsInTableView(tableView: UITableView) ->
  Int {:** This returns the number of sections for the table. Sections are the alphabetical
  sections you see in your contact list. When you aren't using them (you're not now), you
  can just have this function return 1.

With these three methods in place, your code is almost ready to run. You need to make one
change, though. Because you deleted your original view and loaded a new view, you need to
tell this new view to use the `ViewController.swift` file. You did this in the previous example
for the detail view. Do you remember how to do it? Open the storyboard and select the view
controller by clicking the view controller button on the top bar area of the view. In the sidebar
toolbar area, make sure you select the Identity inspector, which is the third button from the
left. For the class, choose `ViewController` from the drop-down shown in Figure 12.14.

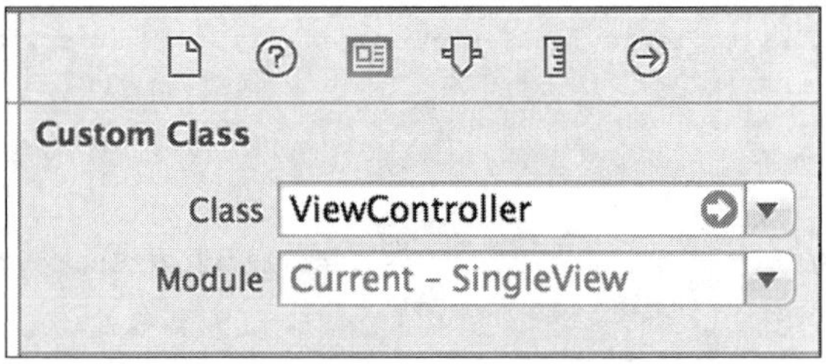

Figure 12.14   Assigning the view a class.

Now if you run the code, you should have a table with three items in it, as shown in Figure
12.15.

Figure 12.15   The table with three items in it.

To format the money amounts so they look correct, open the view controller code, and rewrite the line that sets the detailed text as follows:

```
cell.detailTextLabel?.text = String(format:"$ %.2f",cars[indexPath.row].worth)
```

Here you are using a string formatter to make sure there are always two decimal places when formatting money.

Loading Data from a URL

To load data into a table, you could grab the data from a URL. The following is a small class that you could use to load the JSON data. Create a new file, name it Get.swift, and enter the following in it:

```
import Foundation

class Get {
    class func JSON(url:String,callback:(NSDictionary)->()) {
        requestJSON(url,callback)
    }
    class func requestJSON(url:String,callback:(NSDictionary)->()) {
        var nsURL = NSURL(string: url)
        let task = NSURLSession.sharedSession().dataTaskWithURL(nsURL) {
            (data,response,error) in
            var error:NSError?
            var response = NSJSONSerialization.JSONObjectWithData(data,
                options: NSJSONReadingOptions.MutableContainers, error:
                &error) as NSDictionary
            callback(response)
        }
        task.resume()
    }
}
```

How does this class work? You created two type methods, which can be called as follows:

```
Get.JSON("http://someurl.com") {
  (response) in
  // got data back, let's do something.
}
```

You call the Get.JSON() with a URL, and ending with a trailing closure. Once the data gets inside that closure, you have the response available to you as an NSDictionary.

You could write this in your `viewDidLoad` method. If you wanted to then reload the table with your new data, you could do something like this:

```
Get.JSON("http://someurlwithjsondata.com") {
  (response) in
  for car in response["cars"]!{
    car.append(car)
  }
  dispatch_async(dispatch_get_main_queue()) {
      println("reloading")
      self.tableView.reloadData()
  }
}
```

You must call `dispatch_async` because you must make any changes to the UI on the main thread. By using `dispatch_async`, you can put things on the main thread by specifying the main thread with `dispatch_get_main_queue()`. You can use the reload table function of the table view to reload the table, which will call all the necessary functions once again.

Summary

Many libraries are available that will load your data from a URL. You can easily use one of those libraries along with your knowledge of how to write Swift.

All the user interface controls in Xcode using Swift have specific ways of doing things. In this chapter you took a look at a couple of these, and there are many more different controls available. After you know the way that Apple wants you to write your code, it becomes easier to customize controls. When you are able to build a basic app using the methods described in this chapter, you'll find it easy to take someone else's idea and turn it into an app without much issue. Everyone's going to be coming to you now with their great app ideas. And you will be ready to create those apps.

Index

Numbers

REGISTER

THIS PRODUCT

informit.com/register

Register the Addison-Wesley, Exam Cram, Prentice Hall, Que, and Sams products you own to unlock great benefits.

To begin the registration process, simply go to **informit.com/register** to sign in or create an account. You will then be prompted to enter the 10- or 13-digit ISBN that appears on the back cover of your product.

Registering your products can unlock the following benefits:

- Access to supplemental content, including bonus chapters, source code, or project files.
- A coupon to be used on your next purchase.

Registration benefits vary by product. Benefits will be listed on your Account page under Registered Products.

About InformIT — THE TRUSTED TECHNOLOGY LEARNING SOURCE

INFORMIT IS HOME TO THE LEADING TECHNOLOGY PUBLISHING IMPRINTS Addison-Wesley Professional, Cisco Press, Exam Cram, IBM Press, Prentice Hall Professional, Que, and Sams. Here you will gain access to quality and trusted content and resources from the authors, creators, innovators, and leaders of technology. Whether you're looking for a book on a new technology, a helpful article, timely newsletters, or access to the Safari Books Online digital library, InformIT has a solution for you.

informIT.com

THE TRUSTED TECHNOLOGY LEARNING SOURCE

Addison-Wesley | Cisco Press | Exam Cram
IBM Press | Que | Prentice Hall | Sams

SAFARI BOOKS ONLINE

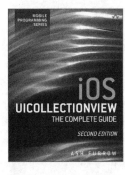